A TRAILS BOOK

WISCONSIN FAMILY WEEKENDS

20 FUN TRIPS FOR YOU AND THE KIDS

SUSAN LAMPERT SMITH

TRAILS BOOKS
Black Earth, Wisconsin

Library of Congress Catalog Card Number: 00-107050
ISBN: 0–915024-86-1

Editor: Stan Stoga
Cover Design: Kathie Campbell
Photos: Susan Lampert Smith (except where noted)
Cover Photo: Michael Shedlock

Printed in the United States of America.
06 05 04 03 02 01 00   6 5 4 3 2 1

The puzzles on pages 17, 31, 66, 91, 101, 114, 121, 128, and 137
are created with Puzzlemaker at Discoveryschool.com

Trails Books, a division of Trails Media Group, Inc.
P.O. Box 317   •   Black Earth, WI 53515
(800) 236–8088   •   e-mail: info@wistrails.com
www.trailsbooks.com

contents

To my adventurous kids,
Ben and Lily

introduction

Wisconsin is a great weekend state—and for families that's really good news. Family leisure time is more fragmented than ever, crammed into the few days that don't conflict with work, school, hockey practice, and piano recitals. Fortunately, all you need is a day or two and you can be off on an adventure.

Think of it, if you live in the upper Midwest, you're just a few hours away from lolling on a Great Lakes beach, cruising down the Mississippi like Huck and Tom, enjoying the solitude of the North Woods, or relishing the urban excitement of one of Milwaukee's great ethnic festivals. And, of course, you're close to some of the world's best trout streams and little sandy lakes.

All of the vacations in this book have been kid tested. (And so have I. Figure that for every chapter, there have been two back-seat sibling fights, three emergency bathroom stops, and 20 choruses of "Are We There Yet?") Kid testing is important because kids don't always like what experts (and tourism boosters) think they will. One of our kids' fondest vacation memories is five rainy days spent canoeing through the North Woods. I remember mounds of wet clothes and long days spent in tiny tents; they remember picking blueberries for breakfast and a big northern pike they named "Bob Dole." They were great on that sodden vacation, but horrible at "The Happiest Place on Earth," the mouse place down in sunny Florida, where they whined, begged, fought, and cried. So go figure.

My advice on family vacations is that simpler is better, and that Wisconsin family vacations are simple. Be sure to leave time for goofing around, poking through gift shops, and eating ice cream cones that melt faster than you can eat them. Childhood is like that ice cream cone—it disappears before your eyes. So make some space in that busy family life to enjoy weekend adventures with your kids while they're still kids.

I'd like to thank my husband, Matthew, for the times he left the farm to go on adventures with us, and the times he had to stay behind. Also, thanks go to my able editors on this project, and all our family and friends who shared vacations and vacation stories with us: the Blackmans, Burmeisters, Greens, Halls, Flahertys, Goplins, Joneses, Liebmanns, Markins, Maroneys, Mitmans, Pohles, Schreiners, Seelys, and Sutters.

section 1
The Northeast

Door County

Imagine a resort where you can take a bike loop that takes you from a marsh full of herons to a lighthouse to a beach where you can buy an ice cream cone and rent a goofy but fun water bike.

Then you can head back to your home in the woods, have dinner, grab a blanket and head to the nearby theater for an evening of rollicking original music and entertainment that everyone in the family will enjoy. The next day you might consider hiking, golfing, taking a trip to a private island paradise, and coming back to watch the sun sink into Lake Michigan at the end of another perfect day.

Peninsula State Park

You can do all those things—and more—without leaving the 3,776 acres of Peninsula State Park. No wonder it's the state's most popular park—and the kind of place where families come back year after year. And if you do leave the park by either the north or south gate, you're right in the middle of Door County's gold coast. Others pay upwards of $1,000 a week to be near the shops, restaurants, and attractions that you're enjoying for the price of state park camping.

So what's fun for kids to do at Peninsula? Biking the miles of trails is a great family activity. If you didn't bring your own bike, you can visit the two rental shops right outside the gate in Fish Creek. Afternoon rental of one adult bike and one child's coaster bike costs $25 for an afternoon from Nor-Door Sports. You can take a 6-mile loop that will take you out the peninsula to the lighthouse. Just after passing Weborg Marsh, you may want to detour off the trail at Weborg Point—a nice spot for fishing, picnicking, and watching the sailboats heading out from Fish Creek.

The Eagle Bluff lighthouse might be more interesting to the adults than the kids, who are eager to move on to Nicolet Beach. Although most of Peninsula's 7 miles of shore is rocky, Nicolet Bay features a crescent of sand, shallow water, and hundreds of people there to enjoy it. Kids don't mind, and actually seem to prefer, having fun with hundreds of others, having seen enough of nature and solitude on the trails.

Nicolet Bay features a snack bar where children deprived of junk food by camping can get pizza, popcorn, and ice cream cones. The park also rents water bikes, paddle boats (not as cool, according to kids), kayaks, canoes, and wind-surfing boards. Be aware, however, that the bay is a popular visiting and mooring spot for motorboats, jet skis, and all sorts of watercraft, so kids need to keep their eyes open while they're trying out that water bike.

On the way back, if you have the energy, climb the Eagle Tower and explore the cliff side trail and caves nearby. If you're in the park in the evening, be sure to visit the American Folklore Theater, located in an open-air amphitheater near the beach. Even kids without much live theater experience are likely to enjoy the antics and silly songs of such original hits as "Lumberjacks in Love" and "Belgians in Heaven." Don't be surprised to hear kids reprising the songs in the car on the way home.

Two Other Great Parks

One good day trip from Peninsula is a trip across the Door Peninsula to Whitefish Dunes State Park. Why drive from one park to the other? Well, the beaches on the Lake Michigan side are generally sandy, while the ones on the

There's always a place to get off the bikes and enjoy the cool lake air when you're biking at Peninsula State Park.

bay side are stony. At Whitefish, you'll see a clearly marked area where rip currents are a problem, and a much longer stretch of sandy beach that's perfect for wading and swimming. Most of the dunes are off-limits, but you can climb Old Baldy, the tallest dune on Lake Michigan's west shore. If there's a naturalist tour, take it to learn a lot more about the dunes.

At the north end of the state park, you'll find Cave Point County Park where the waves make weird crashing sounds beneath the ledges of the point. If it's too rough to swim at the beach, check out Cave Point instead.

But what can you do in Door County with the kids if it rains? Don't give up on the five state parks (Peninsula, Whitefish Dunes, Potawatomi, Newport, and Rock Island) because many of the naturalist programs take place indoors or regardless of weather (like a rainy walk to discover the edible and medicinal plants on Rock Island or an indoor visit with a falcon at Whitefish Dunes.) Other neat nature programs include a special presentation on shipwrecks at one of Peninsula's shelters and a regular Friday night poetry reading on the beach at Newport. Call your favorite park for a schedule.

Ferry to Washington Island

Another rainy day adventure is taking the ferry across "Death's Door" to Washington Island. While the waves toss the ferry, you can explain how many ships went down in this 6-mile passage between Green Bay and the main lake. (There were 100 shipwrecks in the Death's Door passage in 1872 alone.) It costs $40 round-trip to take a car, two adults, and two children over to Washington Island for the day.

Once on the island, you can take tours on the Cherry Train, a string of carts hooked together and pulled behind a car with a loudspeaker. The 22-square-mile island is just the right size for bike adventures, and bike rentals are available at the ferry dock. (Or bring your bike over from the mainland—it's $3 round-trip for a bike, versus $17 for a car.)

Kids like to play with the smooth rounded rocks of Schoolhouse Beach on Washington Harbor. (But don't take them—it's against the law due to people filching rocks to make fireplaces.) Good kid-friendly dining can be had at the Albatross, an old-fashioned drive-in with homemade blueberry malts. There's a covered patio, an outdoor jukebox, and a sandbox to keep the little ones occupied while their burgers are frying. A sign at the window warns of slow service, urging people to slow down now that they're "north of the Tension Line."

The Sailor's Pub restaurant at the Shipyard Marina on Detroit Harbor has good food and waterfront dining. Kids won't want to eat the newly dead fish, but they will like checking out the catch of the day at KK Fiske's in "downtown" Washington Island. Ask the folks at KK Fiske's why they call those ugly fish "lawyers." At Nelsen Hall, you can join the Bitter's Club by tossing down a shot of Angostura Bitters, a tradition that has its roots in Prohibition. (Hey, it's a history lesson for the kids.)

3

Getting to Rock Island State Park is half the fun. Here, the ferry is loaded and ready to leave Jackson Harbor on Washington Island for the 15-minute ride to Rock Island.

Some families make a day trip to Rock Island, another island just beyond Washington Island, accessible by taking the Karfi passenger ferry from Jackson Harbor on Washington Island's Northeast corner. It's not cheap, costing another $8 per person to take this ferry, but some families go for the day to visit Rock Island's fabulous beaches and dunes. Just remember that the last ferry off Rock Island leaves at 4:15 P.M., so don't drowse at the beach or you'll lose your ride. The Icelandic boat house hall on Rock Island is worth a visit, and you can play cards at the tables in the balcony if the weather is bad.

Orchards and Walks

Back on the mainland, you can stop at the orchard and farmer's markets to pick up fresh produce and other treats. We like the Seaquist Orchard store north of Sister Bay. They have plenty of dried cherries, jam samples, and other snacks to try. Don't leave without a warm cherry pie and some coffee (or cherry cider) for the road.

Once you're warm and full, explain to the kids that nature walks can be fun if it's not raining too hard. We like to go up the lake side of the peninsula just north of Baileys Harbor along Highway Q. There you can explore the Ridges Sanctuary and the adjacent Toft Point, which is owned by the University of

Wisconsin-Green Bay. Both have miles of trails under huge pines and other remnants of the Boreal forest that clothed the peninsula after the ice age.

Further up Highway Q, you can turn on Cana Island Road to enjoy the walk out to the pretty Cana Island lighthouse. Most kids can manage the walk out a rocky causeway to the lighthouse. Tell the kids that the white steel covering the tower isn't just for decoration. About 100 years ago, a fierce storm damaged the lighthouse, so the steel was added to protect the brick, which is still underneath.

What's Cooking in the Door

The Town Hall Bakery in Jacksonport is also a cozy place to spend a morning, especially one darkened with rain. Old flowered tablecloths decorate the tables, and the perfume of fresh caramel rolls and lilt of folk music fill the air.

Back in Baileys Harbor, you can warm up over whitefish chowder and pie at the Sandpiper restaurant, or go to Weisgerber's Pub for fish. Our other favorite Door County place for perch is the Greenwood Supper Club, located mid-peninsula at the intersection of Highways F and A. It has neat old paintings of Door County's natural wonders, great lake perch, and, of course, cherry pie for dessert.

Many Door County restaurants offer fish boils. Look for ones, such as the Sandpiper, that do their boils outside so kids can watch. Most kids love it when the flames shoot up around the kettle and the fish boils over, however many, after watching the entertainment of the cooking, won't touch the fish.

When It's Raining

Don't let rain spoil your Door experience. You could pass the time at the movie theater in Sturgeon Bay. Children might also like the Door County Maritime Museum, which features exhibits on boat building and an interactive pilothouse, where children can pretend to be piloting a big ship across one of the stormy Great Lakes.

Nearby on Michigan Street, near the old bridge, Perry's Cherry Diner, with a 1950s motif and homemade ice cream treats, is child and family friendly.

Finally, if it won't quit raining, take down your tent at the state park and head to a real resort—the kind with hot showers, real beds, and cable TV. There are literally dozens to choose from in Door County.

One family-friendly place is the Wagon Trail Resort, located far up the peninsula on Rowley Bay, which has cottages and a main lodge with an indoor pool and sauna. It has rental boats and canoes and is a good launching spot for exploring the nearby Mink River estuary, one of Wisconsin's premier natural areas. But the best thing that the Wagon Trail has to offer is a bakery and restaurant called Grandma's that specializes in Swedish pancakes and huge cinnamon rolls. After you've been camping for a week in the rain, you deserve a warm cinnamon roll at Grandma's.

THINGS TO SEE AND DO

American Folklore Theater (in Peninsula State Park), (920) 868-9999.
Door County Maritime Museum, 120 N. Madison Ave., Sturgeon Bay,
     (920) 743-5958, www.dcmm.org.
Edge of the Park Bike Rental, Fish Creek, (920) 868-3344.
Nicolet Bay Boat and Bike Rentals (in Peninsula State Park),
     (920) 854-9220.
Nor-Door Sports and Cyclery, Fish Creek, (920) 868-2275.
Peninsula State Park Golf Course, (920) 854-5791.
Ridges Sanctuary, Highway Q, Baileys Harbor, (920) 839-2802.
Sturgeon Bay Cinemas, North 18th Ave., Sturgeon Bay, (920) 743-3569.
Whitefish Dunes State Park, 3701 Clark Lake Rd., Sturgeon Bay,
     (920) 823-2400.

PLACES TO STAY

Peninsula State Park, Fish Creek, (920) 868-3258.
Wagon Trail Resort, 1041 Highway ZZ, Ellison Bay, 54210,
     (800) 99-WAGON, www.wagontrail.com.

PLACES FOR FOOD

Albatross Drive-In, Main Rd., Washington Island, (920) 847-2203.
Greenwood Supper Club, Highways A & F, Fish Creek, (920) 839-2451.
KK Fiske's (home of the "fish mortician"), Washington Island, Main Rd.,
     (920) 847-2121.
Perry's Cherry Diner, 230 Michigan St., Sturgeon Bay, (920) 743-9910.
Sailor's Pub, South Shore Dr., Washington Island, (920) 847-2105.
Sandpiper Restaurant, Highway 57, Baileys Harbor, (920) 839-2528.
Seaquist Orchards, Highway 42, Sister Bay, (920) 854-4199.
Town Hall Bakery, 6225 Highway 57, Jacksonport, (920) 823-2116.
Weisgerber's Pub, Highway 57, Baileys Harbor, (920) 839-9001.

Green Bay

When the idea of Green Bay is suggested as a weekend destination, expect some mixed reactions from the family. Non-football fans will likely roll their eyes, but true cheeseheads will be thrilled. This is because everyone will immediately think Packers. But the city and the surrounding area have more than enough other attractions to keep the weekend from being Lambeau-dominated.

Bay Beach Park

Bay Beach Amusement Park is the kind of place that sends a thrill down the spines of cheapskate parents.

Your children get out of the car and gape open-mouthed at the rides arrayed in this park along Bay Beach Road on Green Bay's east side. You wave your hands magnanimously and say, "Go ahead, live it up. Go on every ride as many times as you like."

"As many times as we want?" ask the confused children, used to strict budgets and long lectures about "how much money we spend on you ungrateful children."

"As many times as you want," you say.

After an hour and a half, the bill will stand at about $3. In truth, it's tough to spend $10 in an afternoon at Bay Beach. Bay Beach is a rarity: a city-owned amusement park where the goal is affordable family fun. Ride tickets cost 20 cents apiece and the most expensive rides are two tickets. That's 40 cents, for those of you keeping track at home.

The rides at Bay Beach include carnival favorites such as bumper cars, Tilt-a-Whirl, Scrambler, a giant slide, and a centrifugal force ride called Scat. Many of the rides are designed for little children, including a train ride around the park, a merry-go-round, and boat and Jeep rides, all of which cost only 20 cents each.

The only ride that costs more is the pony ride, at $1. Bring swimsuits for the kids because there's a free wading pool with little slides. Even the food is cheap. A hamburger will set you back $1, and the most expensive soft drink is $1.

The "Yo-Yo" ride at Bay Beach thrills kids with its bird's-eye view of the amusement park and Green Bay—and thrills parents with its low cost.

With all these bargains, Bay Beach draws children like honey draws flies. You'll meet families who are in for the day from a wide radius that takes in Wausau, the Fox Cities, and Manitowoc. Some afternoons, it seems as though every day care in northeastern Wisconsin is at Bay Beach. So instead of paying with money, you pay with time spent in long lines, especially on the weekends.

The park has been a Green Bay institution for generations; you'll meet grandparents who played here as children and dreamed of growing up to be the train conductor at Bay Beach. The park attracts more than a million visitors a year, and holds teen nights and big-band dances at its waterfront pavilion. There's a nature center across the street, with education programs about the wildlife of Green Bay and 5 miles of hiking trails.

Bay Beach is open weekends from early May to the end of September, with varying hours. From late May until the end of August, it is open daily from 10 A.M. to 9 P.M. It's easy to find: from Interstate 43 in downtown Green Bay, take the Webster Avenue exit north towards the lake. You'll see the park, which is on your left on Bay Beach Road.

Pilgrimage to Packerland

Little kids may want to grow up to drive the Bay Beach train, but older kids in Wisconsin want to grow up to be a Green Bay Packer. Kids can live out this fantasy—even try on Brett Favre's shoes—at the Green Bay Packers complex on Lombardi Avenue.

Many Packer fan families plan their pilgrimages around Packer training camp which begins in late July and runs through late August. With tickets at Lambeau Field so difficult to come by, summer training camp is the only chance many kids will ever have to see their heroes in the flesh.

Back in the olden days (before the Packers' 1997 Super Bowl victory), Packer training camp was truly a low-key, hometown affair. Kids with bikes would wait outside the Lambeau Field locker rooms and lend their bikes to Packers who pedaled across the parking lot to the Oneida Street practice field, looking like giant circus clowns on tricycles. The kids would jog along behind the bikes, carrying their heroes' helmets.

Fans could sit inside the practice field on lawn chairs, and those who didn't fit would stand along the chain link fence on Oneida Street, craning for a view of some lineman's huge body or Favre's red jersey. Afterwards, kids would swarm the players for autographs as they made their way back to Lambeau to shower and change. And that's when things started getting ugly. Adult autograph seekers (some of them eager to resell the autographs) would shove kids aside or actually pay children to procure autographs from players who favored children over adults. It was a stressful scene that resulted in more than one crying child and more than one angry, tired Packer.

Something had to change and now the Packer training camp has become a more regimented and commercial affair. The kids still lend their bikes to Packers, but after practice, the team makes certain Packers available to sign autographs. You don't know who it will be (usually a mix of stars and rookies). Tickets to the autograph session are handed out in the crowd during practice in a random manner. You must have one to get autographs, so keep your eyes peeled for the person handing out tickets. Fortunately, this system is less chaotic and the Packers stay until every kid has their autographs.

The Packers have also begun selling tickets to the entire training camp experience. The training camp package includes a reserved seat at either morning or afternoon practice (generally 8:45 A.M. and 2:15 P.M., but call ahead), a ticket to the Packers Experience, and either a tour of Lambeau Field or a visit to the Packer Hall of Fame.

Is the $15 ticket worth it? Yes, and no. The best seat at practice is the lawn chair you bring yourself—and you can still set it up for free if you get there early enough to snag a spot. On the other hand, you can plan a trip to training camp, only to never see the Packers because practice has been cancelled or moved inside due to bad weather. (The indoor Don Hutson Center is not open to the public.) So, at least the other tours give you a chance to feel like you are a part of the Packers. Of the three options, the tour of Lambeau on little golf cart

Kids of all ages enjoy visiting the Packer Hall of Fame and seeing the Green Bay Packers at summer training camp.

trains seems the least interesting to kids.

The Green Bay Packer Hall of Fame, across from Lambeau Field, is a better bet. Kids seem to groove on seeing the trophies from Super Bowls I, II, and XXXI. The hall is mostly a chance to relive the past Glory Days of the Packers. Kids who view Reggie White as ancient Packer history may not be impressed. But parents who remember the days of Bart Starr and Ray Nitschke practically turn back into children again when viewing tapes of those old games.

The Hall of Fame gives you a chance to pass on family lore—how you got frostbite at the famous Ice Bowl of 1967, but continued to cheer your Packers to victory despite the $-16°$ F temperatures at the old Frozen Tundra. (Of course you were there! Despite the official Ice Bowl game day attendance of 50,800, millions of Packers fans now claim to have been present when Starr stuck it to the Dallas Cowboys.)

Although parents love the Hall of Fame, children go wild for the Packers Experience in the Arena next door. The indoor-outdoor exhibit (open during training camp and home Packer games) gives kids a chance to run, jump, and kick like real Packers.

Kids can run through an agility course like the one in training camp and have their rocket-like passes timed on a speed clock. They can kick field goals and, like real NFL players, unwind from their stressful workout by playing a round of golf on the miniature putt-putt course.

It can be hilarious to watch little kids try on giant shoulder pads that hang to their knees, while their feet swim in the boat-like shoes of Brett Favre or LeRoy Butler. And, for the video generation, the Packers Experience lets kids

🌲 Purple Packer Pickup

Here's a game that's easy enough for the smallest kids and the most distracted drivers to play. When you're the first to see one of these Wisconsin roadside attractions, you shout it out and score points. And, you may add different vehicles to the list.

First one to 20 points wins. Then start over.

Purple pickup truck with Packer sticker	20 points (automatic win)
Manure spreader	5 points (add a point if operating)
Snowmobile	5 points (add a point if it's June, July, or August)
Volkswagen Bug	1 point
Any vehicle with Packer sticker	1 point

experience Packer games in their favorite way—by playing football video games on a giant screen. It's the kind of place where parents get tired long before children, who generally have to be dragged out.

When You're Hungry

By this point, everyone should be famished and, although Lombardi Avenue is full of chain restaurants, why not take the kids to someplace that is authentically Green Bay? That would be Chili John's. From Lambeau Field, take Lombardi Avenue west toward Highway 41, but before you get to the highway, turn right (north) on Military Avenue. Chili John's is 519 S. Military, near Mason Street.

Chili John's has been a Green Bay institution for nearly a century and people who move away (including some former Packers, we're told) miss it so much they have it mail-ordered to them. The original Chili John was John Isaac, a Lithuanian who immigrated to Green Bay. In 1913 he opened a shop at the Main Street bridge with a sign that read, simply, "Chili."

The beauty of Chili John's is that each dish is prepared to order, made on a base of chili that ranges from mild to extra hot. You can have super hot chili meat with beans and raw onions, while your kids can eat the mild version with no beans, on top a pile of spaghetti and topped with a mountain of oyster crackers. It's cheap and filling, and thus the perfect family meal. (Except, perhaps, for families who have to endure a long car ride home together.)

For families interested in fine dining, a great place to take kids is Pier 64 (formerly Hullo's on the Fox), located in downtown Green Bay, on the Fox River. There are docks out back where people arriving by boat can berth, and the nautical theme is carried on throughout the restaurant. The first thing kids see when they enter is a giant boat filled with peanuts in the shell for pre-dinner munching. There's a room with a giant chalkboard wall for doodlers and an outdoor sand area where children can play while their parents enjoy cocktails on the patio. The staff is extremely friendly and wears goofy fishing vest ensembles. Despite the wild atmosphere, the seafood and other dinner specials are excellent.

Other Attractions

Another kid-worthy attraction in the Green Bay area is the Children's Museum which is geared toward little children and located in the Port Plaza Mall in downtown Green Bay.

The NEW Zoo is located 11 miles northwest of Green Bay near Suamico. Take Highway 41 north to the Highway B exit, then go 2 miles west, and a mile north on Highway IR to the NEW Zoo. The name refers both to the fact that it's the zoo of northeastern Wisconsin and to the recent face-lift the facilities have undergone. The zoo features hiking and nature trails, a picnic area, and educational programs. Admission is $2 for adults and $1 for children.

Families that want to learn more about the Oneida people can visit the Oneida Nation Museum on the reservation or the Neville Public Museum in downtown Green Bay.

And no family visit to Wisconsin's oldest city would be complete without telling the story of the "discovery" of Wisconsin. You can take your kids to the historic site, Red Banks, located about 7 miles northeast of Green Bay on Highway 57, on the way to Door County.

There's a little wayside on the side of the road with a statue of the French-Canadian explorer Jean Nicolet. Nicolet was trying to discover a trade route through the Great Lakes to China when he landed here, wearing silk robes, shooting pistols, and speaking Chinese to the bemused Ho-Chunk Indian villagers. The Ho-Chunk took the explorer in and held a large feast in his honor.

The story proves that, much like Nicolet's expedition to China, family vacations can work out alright even if they don't turn out as planned.

Lodging Options

Green Bay is full of hotels and motels. If you want to stay as close as possible to the hallowed ground of Lambeau Field, there are a number of hotels in the immediate area.

For a truly different lodging experience, consider the Radisson Hotel, which is owned by the Oneida Nation and located across from Austin-Straubel Field, Green Bay's airport. Take Highway 172 west from Highway 41 to find the airport and hotel.

The hotel has a Native American theme, an airy lobby, and an indoor pool. Kids can learn about the history of the tribe, eat Native American foods, such as wild rice soup, in the restaurant, and check out the turtle-shaped fountain that symbolizes the tribe. Just beyond the fountain, kids can see the reason for this glitzy hotel and the rest of the tribe's new wealth—the flashing lights of the Oneida Casino, connected to the hotel. Children aren't allowed inside, but gambling does provide for some interesting parent-child conversations on the way home.

THINGS TO SEE AND DO

Bay Beach Park, 1660 E. Shore Dr., Green Bay, (920) 391-3671.

Children's Museum of Green Bay, Port Plaza Mall, (920) 432-GEXP.

Green Bay Packer Hall of Fame (and stadium tours) 855 Lombardi Ave., (888) 442-7225.

Packers Experience (next to Hall of Fame), (920) 494-9507. Packer training camp fan packages (late July to late August) are on sale at the Packer Hall of Fame, Brown County Arena, and the Packer ticket office. Call (800) 895-0071. Also check the official Packers Web site for training camp schedules and other information, www.packers.com.

Oneida Museum, W892 EE Rd., Oneida, (920) 869-2768.

Neville Public Museum, 210 Museum Place, Green Bay, (920) 448-4460.

PLACES TO STAY

Baymont Inn, 2840 S. Oneida St., Green Bay, (920) 494-7887.

Country Inn & Suites by Carlson, 2945 Allied St., Green Bay, (920) 336-6600.

Days Inn-Lambeau Field, 1978 Holmgren Way, Green Bay, (920) 498-8088.

Fairfield Inn by Marriott., 2850 S. Oneida St., Green Bay, (920) 497-1010.

Hilton Garden Inn, 1015 Lombardi Ave., Green Bay, (920) 405-0400.

Radisson Inn, 2040 Airport Dr., Green Bay, (920) 494-7300.

Super 8 Motel, 2868 S. Oneida St., Green Bay, (920) 494-2042.

PLACES FOR FOOD

Chili John's, 519 S. Military Rd., Green Bay, (920) 494-4624.

Pier 64, 1350 Marine St., Green Bay, (920) 435-4855.

Manitowoc, Two Rivers, and Beyond

Many families make Manitowoc a jumping off spot for a cruise across Lake Michigan aboard the SS *Badger,* the car ferry that crosses between Manitowoc and Ludington, Michigan, shaving 420 miles and the dreaded Chicago traffic off the trip around the lake.

In Manitowoc

Before hopping the ferry, note that there's enough to do in Manitowoc, a friendly city "down by the lake" (as the Germanic locals say), that it's worth lingering here on Wisconsin's east coast. (And if you're staying before you cruise, ask your hotel about complimentary shuttles to the ferry.)

For one thing, children and dads, especially, will want to tour the real World War II vintage submarine at the Wisconsin Maritime Museum located on the waterfront next to the Inn on Maritime Bay. The museum pays homage to the city's shipbuilding tradition—during World War II, the city's ship yards cranked out 28 submarines, and the sports teams at Manitowoc's Lincoln High School are still called the Ships.

Kids, especially those who have seen a few World War II movies, get a kick out of imagining life below the waves in the incredibly cramped crew's quarters as the klaxon warns of an imminent dive. (Except, of course, claustrophobics, who break out into a sweat when they hear, "Dive! Dive!") Other displays show how ships are built and depict Wisconsin's long history of shipbuilding. (Don't forget—one of those guys on the Wisconsin state flag is a sailor.)

When you're done admiring the ships, walk a block to Beerntsen's, an old time candy shop and ice cream parlor on Eighth Street, where you can eat your hot fudge sundae in wooden booths that date back to the 1930s. Beerntsen's sells homemade candies, and during the holiday season, you can buy hard candy icicles, ribbons, candy canes, and wired cherries for decorating your tree.

Other notable kid-friendly eateries include Late's, an old-fashioned barbecue and hamburger stand near Lincoln High School—take your bag of burgers across the street for a lakefront picnic at Red Arrow Park. And out on Calumet Avenue (business Highway 42 & 151) is the Penguin, a venerable custard stand and drive-in with one of the best vintage signs left in the state.

As fishermen know, Manitowoc is also the jumping off point for fishing charters for those in search of giant Lake Michigan salmon and lake trout. If you have a kid who likes fishing and has the attention span to spend a long day on a fishing boat, a charter is worth considering. The growth of charter fishing in the last 25 years has been responsible for the huge boom in lakefront marinas in the area. Even kids who don't fish will enjoy looking at the boats.

Two Rivers— Ice Cream and History

After spending some quality time in Manitowoc, it's time to head north along the Lake Michigan shore for about 5 miles to Two Rivers. Here, kids will find the answer to the trivia question, "Where was the ice cream sundae invented?" (And, they'll learn why this treat has a funny spelling.) The treat was invented in 1881 at Berner's Ice Cream parlor, when owner Edward Berner doctored up a dish of ice cream with the syrup that had been used for sodas. The treat was sold only on Sundays, until, as legend has it, a little girl asked Berner to "pretend" it was Sunday. The weird spelling came from a glassware salesman who misspelled the name as "Sundae" on an order for dishes.

The original Berner's is long gone, but the Two Rivers Historical Society has done a nice job recreating a vintage ice cream parlor for those who like their historical facts sweetened with a bit of reality. It's located beneath the giant hanging sundae sign at the Washington House, 1622 Jefferson Street, one of three historical museums located along Jefferson Street, in the shadow of the Hamilton Beach plant.

History buffs have their choice of ice cream and toppings, all served up in a tulip glass dish. But don't be surprised if they're also interested in poking through the other

For history that tastes wonderful, don't miss Ed Berner's Ice Cream Parlor at 17th and Jefferson in Two Rivers, a replica of the place where the ice cream sundae was born in Two Rivers in 1881.

15

rooms of the historic rooming house hotel. There are displays of historic toys and a fabulous, fully furnished Victorian dollhouse that little girls of all ages will dream about. The society also operates a museum in a former convent down the street at 1810 Jefferson Street and a museum of old wooden printing type across the street at 1619 Jefferson Street.

Across the river, kids will like exploring the Rogers Street Fishing Village, which includes two fishing vessels, four fishing sheds, and the lighthouse that guarded the Two Rivers harbor from 1886 until the 1960s. The French-Canadian village is listed on the National Register of Historic Places.

Next door, the kids with an adventure streak should check out the U.S. Coast Guard museum which has displays on lifesaving and artifacts recovered from some of the state's most deadly shipwrecks. (Of course, if you're planning a ferry crossing, you might want to whisk the kids past all the shipwreck stuff.)

North along the Lakeshore

North of Two Rivers about 6 miles, but still in Manitowoc County, is Point Beach State Forest, a great place to camp or have a daily beach adventure. The 5-mile long beach can trick you into thinking you're not on the east coast of Wisconsin, but on the East Coast of the United States, looking out at the Atlantic Ocean. The campsites are wooded and fairly private, and early risers can watch the sun rise up out of the lake.

The next day you can loll at the beach—kids like to collect those flat smooth Lake Michigan stones and embellish them with paint and markers. We've found that tubes of "glitter glue" are excellent for decorating rocks and that you can make your own "rock checkers" set or create a decorated rock treasure chest. Have a building contest and see who can build the neatest rock castle.

Once you've had enough of the beach, you can set off in search of educational adventures. For the kids that want to know how electricity comes out of the wall, a stop at the Energy Center at the Point Beach Nuclear Power Plant might be in order. The education center was closed for remodeling during 1999 but is supposed to reopen with modern, hands-on displays. (If it's like the old center, parents may want to counter the pro-nuclear rhetoric with a few explanations about the problems of nuclear power.)

A Short Trip West

Those who are interested in seeing how the area's Bohemian, German, and Norwegian pioneers lived may like the historical village, Pinecrest, located in the hills of western Manitowoc County. Kids especially like the old General Store, and Pinecrest offers a variety of special programs through the year, such as a blacksmith demonstration on Father's Day and a program on how cooking was done in the olden days on Mother's Day.

Wild Wisconsin Rivers

J C M M E M E Z B U N N V E F

O H F F G T K F N W M R E L L

Z J W P A O O O K C A L B U A

V U G R C D G J A M M F A R M

P B H N F A K T A N R Y S B B

V E S V K B W L L K U D F N E

H M S E K I C K A P O O Y M A

B F M H H N R C A E B D Q C U

G A O X T K H E Q F L W K B V

N A E X C I F V V R O C K Y Y

G H H Y P L G S A E D U E M F

K B E P O I L O V D F X U A K

X M E W A G A P O D Z Y B K H

D W L S B X F H B V P W K Z E

A I T B P F Q U Q Y I J I U G

BLACK	BRULE	CHIPPEWA
FEVER	FLAMBEAU	FOX
KICKAPOO	NAMEKAGON	PESHTIGO
ROCK	WOLF	

(Solution on page 142)

Farther west, but definitely worth a visit if you're in the area on a Thursday, Friday, or Saturday, is the Kaytee Avian Education Center in Chilton, about 25 miles west of Manitowoc on Highway 151. Look for the signs on the eastern edge of Chilton. Opened in 1995 by the locally owned bird seed company, the center is a wonderful place for children and adults to learn about birds.

The place is a hotspot with school groups, and the staff is especially patient with children. Your children will get to hold tropical birds and watch them perform tricks. The rainforest exhibit is like a smaller version of the free-flying rainforest at the Milwaukee Zoo. Children are delighted at the parakeets who have figured out how to get out of the wires meant to keep them corralled.

Kids who have a thing for animals may have to be dragged away from the windows of the nursery where newly-hatched baby birds are kept. If your timing is right, you'll be able to see the staff hand-feeding the babies.

The center also has a series of excellent hands-on displays that allow children to identify birds by their calls, make bird footprints in sand, and study feathers under a microscope. An educational film shown in the center's theater helps children understand how the rainforests of the Tropics and the east coast of Wisconsin are connected by the birds who migrate between the two.

On the boat trip to Michigan, don't be surprised if one child is nagging for a pet bird while the other is mimicking the funny caws and sayings of Smurf, the center's giant macaw.

Back to Manitowoc and Across the Lake

Some families wonder if crossing Lake Michigan on the SS *Badger* is really worth the expense.

Well, the literature explains that a four-hour crossing between Manitowoc and Ludington in Michigan cuts 425 miles (and a trip through the freeway jungle of Chicago) off your trip. But when you figure that you need to be at the boat an hour before it leaves (even with reservations) and that the unloading takes nearly that long, you're really not saving much time.

And it's not cheap, either. At 1999 fares, a family of four with two kids between the ages of 5 and 15 would pay $156 just to get themselves and their vehicle to Michigan. Add another $27 if you want to rent a stateroom for the trip.

Most Wisconsin families say it's worth it to make the trip at least once, because it makes such great memories for the kids. You can cut expenses by bringing a cooler filled with drinks and snacks. (Take it out when you board because you can't get into your car once you're underway. Remember, too,

It's "all aboard" the ferry as the SS *Badger* prepares to leave port in Manitowoc. Trips aboard the car ferry make crossing Lake Michigan an adventure for old and young alike.

that if you bring the family pet, it has to stay in your car or in a kennel during the crossing.)

Whether or not you should rent a stateroom probably depends on the age of your kids and the timing of your crossing. For older kids, it's probably not worth the expense. They're so thrilled with being on the boat, playing the free bingo tournaments in the lounge, browsing the gift shop, blowing money in the game arcade, and watching the kids' movies that they couldn't be bribed to go take a nap.

For families with young kids, however, the cabins can be a lifesaver and worth every penny. Where else on a trip can exhausted parents take a nap and wake up 425 miles closer to their destination? The cabins have their own small bathrooms and two single beds. One bed pulls down out of the wall so it can be put away if you want more room. But watch the kids, because they could manage to fold up their little brother in the bed.

In the restaurant, kids can get their drinks in a souvenir SS *Badger* cup with free refills during the journey. The cafeteria serves food that kids will like and parents will tolerate. Sometimes in mid-summer, the crossings are so crowded that it's tough to find a place to eat or sit in the sun. If it's crowded, find out when the kids' movie begins and get there early for seats.

There are chairs on the deck, but remember that even in mid-July, it's very cool in the middle of the lake, so bring jackets and sweaters, even if you won't need them for the rest of your trip.

Finally, hang on to your ticket. The ferry line promises a round-trip discount if you return for a second voyage anytime during the sailing season.

FOR MORE INFORMATION

Manitowoc-Two Rivers Chamber of Commerce. 1515 Memorial Dr., Manitowoc, 54220. (800) 262–7892, www.manitowocchamber.com. Two other useful Web sites are: www.tworiverschamber.com and www.manitowoc.org/tourism/html.

THINGS TO SEE AND DO

Kaytee Avian Education Center, 521 Clay St., Chilton, (800) 669-9580,
www.kaytee.com.

Lake Michigan Car Ferry, Manitowoc, (800) 841-4243, www.ssbadger.com.

Pinecrest Historical Village, Pinecrest Lane, rural Manitowoc, (920)
684–5110. (From I-43 take exit 152 west, Highway JJ to Pinecrest Lane.)

Point Beach Energy Center, 6400 Nuclear Rd., Two Creeks, (920) 755-6400.

Rogers Street Fishing Village and U.S. Coast Guard Museum,
2102 Jackson St., Two Rivers, (920) 793-5905.

Washington House (historic ice cream parlor), 1622 Jefferson St.,
Two Rivers, (920) 793-2490.

Wisconsin Maritime Museum, 75 Maritime Dr., Manitowoc,
(920) 684-0218, www.wimaritimemuseum.org.

PLACES TO STAY

Point Beach State Forest, 9400 Highway O, Two Rivers, (920) 794-7480.

Inn on Maritime Bay, 101 Maritime Dr., Manitowoc, (920) 682-7000.

PLACES FOR FOOD

Beerntsen's Confectionery, 108 N. Eighth St., Manitowoc, (920) 684-9616.

Late's Bar-B-Q Stand, 1924 S. Ninth St., Manitowoc, (920) 682-1539.

The Penguin drive-in, 3900 Calumet Ave., Manitowoc, (920) 684-6403.

Minocqua and the Flambeau Area

Every family has its own sign that it is finally—after all those miles and all those whiney "are we there yet?"s—in the North Woods. Some believe the sign outside Portage, which claims it is the gateway to the north, marks the boundary. Others must pass Highway 10, Highway 8, or the Rhinelander Hodag to know they're truly "Up North."

One Up-North ritual is to begin or end the trip up Highway 39/51 at Bosaki's Boat House in Minocqua. There's something about eating a burger and looking out at the blue water of Minocqua Lake that lets you know you're really Up North. Be sure to ask for a table outside on the deck, and if you're at this Minocqua institution on a Sunday, Wednesday, or Friday in mid-summer, you might be lucky enough to catch a free show by the Min-Aqua Bats water-ski team.

Minocqua—The Basics

Minocqua—with its 24-hour grocery stores and multiplex movie theater—is the downtown of northern Wisconsin, and there's something here for everyone. If you're looking for a place to stay, there are a lot of options. In cool weather, resorts and hotels with indoor pools seem best for fulfilling the desire of children to swim. Two Minocqua Lake resorts—The Pointe, located on the other side of the bridge from Bosaki's, and The Beacons, located across the lake—have pools and condominium units with full kitchens.

And, the area abounds with family restaurants. If your brood is composed of carnivores, you can't do better than the "sirloin burgers" served at the Little Musky Bar on Highway 51 just north of Woodruff. (But vegetarians, beware: meatless offerings are nonexistent.)

Pasta-eating families will like Mama's, an Italian Supper Club located just west of Minocqua on Highway 70. Mama's features a pasta buffet, good homemade pizza, a children's menu, and views of pretty, little Curtis Lake.

For breakfasts and lunches, we've always enjoyed the Island Cafe in downtown Minocqua. There's a great salad and soup bar, as well as homemade pies and milk shakes. Next door, caffeine-addicted parents can tank up on lattes at Horhay's coffee shop.

And finally, if you're looking for true North Woods ambiance, you can't do better than Pope's Gresham Lodge. The little bar has so many stuffed animal trophies that kids probably can't count them all before their dinners arrive. The bar serves an all-you-can-eat, family-style fish fry on Fridays. You order at the bar and are seated when your food is at the table (a blessing for children who don't like to sit and wait). To find Pope's, go about 5 miles north of Woodruff on Highway 51, then turn left on Gresham Road.

Biking and Hiking—South of Minocqua

If you don't want to hang around town and let your children drain your pocketbook in the knick-knack shops, the best thing to do is explore some great area trails. The Bearskin State Trail begins in Minocqua and winds for 18 miles south on an abandoned railroad bed. The trail starts about two blocks west of downtown, near the intersection of Park and Front Street. If you're leaving from Bosaki's, just take Park Street north a few blocks along the shore of Minocqua Lake.

There's no prettier start to a day of biking than the Bearskin Trail bridge, which crosses the lake from Minocqua, the "Island City."

Because the trail starts off on a bridge over Minocqua Lake, the scenery pay-off is immediate. After crossing the lake, you're immediately swallowed up by the North Woods and the trail cuts between a series of small lakes, such as Baker and Bolger. About 6 miles south, you'll come into the Hazelhurst area, where you could stop at one of the trailside establishments—such as Hazelhurst Pub & Grub, the Rustic Inn, or the Cottage Inn—for some refreshments, before heading back into Minocqua.

After biking through this region dotted with lakes, your troops will probably be ready to swim in one to cool off. Torpy Park, located on Highway 51 in downtown Minocqua, has a sandy beach with lifeguards. There are also lifeguards at a nice beach in a more secluded park setting at Brandy Lake in adjacent Woodruff. Go north into Woodruff on Highway 51, turn left (west) at the light at Highway 47, then go right again to Brandy Lake which is just north of Highway 47. It's also a favorite spot to stop for a picnic and a dip if you're heading farther north on Highway 51.

Biking and Hiking—North of Minocqua

If it's the height of summer, you may want to head for the woods. The Northern Highland–American Legion State Forest begins just north of town, and although it's not an official state park, families will find nice, water-edge campgrounds on a number of pristine, little lakes, located between Minocqua and Boulder Junction. You can pick up maps of the campgrounds at the Department of Natural Resources headquarters in Woodruff. To find it, turn east on Highway 47, then left on Highway J.

The forest has 18 campgrounds but just 4—those at Clear, Crystal, Firefly, and Muskellunge Lakes—can be reserved. Reservations are taken up to 11 months in advance by the same service that handles state park reservations.

Crystal Lake, located 5 miles west of Sayner on Highway N, is a nice one for families. Across highway N, you'll find a kid-friendly nature trail around Fallison Lake. The trail is only 1.5 miles long, just right for little legs, but packs in a lot of scenery from hilltop views of the lake to wetlands.

Another more adventurous trail is the one that winds around Pallette and Escanaba Lakes in the Northern Highland State Forest. The entire loop, which also includes the tiny Mystery Lake, is 8 miles, but you can take only the Pallette Lake loop which is just over 1 mile. All these little lakes allow canoeing, so feel free to bring one along. Just remember that Escanaba Lake is part of a fish research project, so you need a special permit (which you can pick up in the parking lot) to fish there. To find Pallette Lake, go north out of Woodruff on Highway 51, then turn right on Highway M towards Boulder Junction. After about 5 miles, turn right on Nebish Road, which will take you into Pallette Lake.

The northern pike grow bigger than babies in the many lakes of the Northern Highland State Forest.

Because you're in the area, you should also check out the beautiful, piney Cathedral Point that separates huge Trout Lake into northern and southern segments. Here, tall white pines grow on the site of an old Indian garden. You'll find the road west to the point just across Highway M from where you turn east on Nebish Road.

Three Museums Not Just for Rainy Days

Kids who've had enough of the North Woods of today might enjoy learning about life back in the olden days. The Dr. Kate Museum, located in a log cabin across Highway 51 from the Lakeland Cinema, is an interesting place to start. The museum teaches kids the story of Dr. Kate Newcomb, "the angel on snowshoes" who would trek through the wilderness to reach patients in need of care.

For some reason, kids are also quite taken with the sign depicting the giant penny, located at the museum. The sign memorializes the "million penny parade," a crusade led by Dr. Kate to get schoolchildren to raise money to build a hospital in Woodruff. Donations poured in from across the country (parents and grandparents who remember the 1950s may well remember raising pennies for Dr. Kate) and Woodruff got its hospital. The story is proof that kids can make a difference.

Another excellent history museum is located on the Lac du Flambeau reservation, about 10 miles northwest of Woodruff on Highway 47. The centerpiece of the George W. Brown Jr. Ojibwa Museum is a circular display that shows the natural seasons of the Ojibwa (Chippewa) year. The museum shows the ice fishing season (using spear and decoys to fish through the ice), the summer maple sugar camp, and the summer fishing and fall hunting camps. Be sure to watch the videos on Ojibwa culture. Kids will be interested in the 300-year-old dugout canoe rescued from one of the reservation lakes and will take a long look at the beadwork.

One display tells a historical detective story. The beaded bandoleer bag with the initials W.A. was discovered for sale by a museum director who was visiting a California gallery. The man recognized it as a traditional Ojibwa design and later found a picture of a Lac du Flambeau man wearing the beaded ornament. The tribe bought the bag back from the dealer—an example of how Indians are attempting to regain treasures that have left their reservations. To find the museum, take Highway 47 to Lac du Flambeau and turn left on Highway D.

The museum also explains that Lac du Flambeau was a major trading port during the fur trade era and part of a system of trails leading to Lake Superior. Kids can see some of the history for themselves if you continue on Highway 47, past Highway D. About a mile farther, on the left, you'll see a historical marker on the shore of Flambeau Lake. It tells of the Battle of Strawberry Island, the last stand of a long-running war between the Sioux, who once occupied this area, and the Ojibwa who were moving in from the Great Lakes. The Ojibwa won the battle of Strawberry Island—which kids can see from the historical marker—and the Sioux were banished west of the Mississippi, to the Dakotas where they live today.

A really cool—according to kids—display of traditional Indian life is the Wa-Swa-Goning village, located on Highway H, less than a mile north of Highway 47. The village is 20 acres on the shores of Moving Cloud Lake, where kids can wander through a village of birch bark wigwams and see traditional methods of drying fish and skins. Kids might recognize the tour guide—Lac du Flambeau member Nick Hockings—who performs and teaches in schools across Wisconsin. His village is a huge hit with European tourists and has been the site of historical movies filmed by the BBC and a Canadian film company. Wa-Swa-Goning is a great spot to visit, but not always open during the week, so call ahead.

How 'bout a Powwow?

Another way to see history come alive is to attend a powwow at the Indian Bowl, located behind the Wa-Swa-Goning museum. The public dances happen regularly in July and August, but call ahead to check the schedule.

If you're lucky enough to be visiting during the second weekend in July, you can take part in the Bear River Powwow, one of the traditional seasons of pow-wows that take place on Wisconsin Indian reservations throughout the summer. Because it draws dancers and musicians from other tribes, as well as many craftspeople and artisans, taking in a real powwow is highly recommended.

In Wisconsin, dancers visit a circuit of annual powwows: the Sakaogon (Mole Lake) Chippewa celebrate the "strawberry moon" with a June powwow, the Oneida powwow is always fourth of July weekend, followed by the Bear River Powwow in Lac du Flambeau, and the Honor the Earth Powwow at Lac Courte Oreilles reservation near Hayward. In late summer, the St. Croix and Bad River bands have wild rice powwows.

Powwow itself is a relatively modern, Pan-Indian celebration. Powwows are friendly, family affairs, with participants ranging from the smallest children to the elders.

For non-Indians who want to understand and take part in a powwow, the key words are honor, respect, and, of course, fry bread.

Each powwow begins with what is known as the "grand entry," a procession led by the Native American veterans carrying staffs of eagle feathers, American flags, and the flags of the branch of the military in which they served. You should stand and remove your hat, as you would for the singing of the national anthem.

If an eagle feather drops during the traditional entry, the ceremony stops, and the feather is blessed. A fallen eagle feather must never be photographed.

This brings us to the second reminder about powwows: respect. The dancers are Wisconsin citizens like you, not actors nor museum objects. Act as you would expect a visitor to your church picnic or family reunion to act. If you would like to take a picture of a dancer, you should ask the dancer first.

Many of the powwow dances are designed to honor groups of tribal people: veterans, youth, elders, mothers, and fathers. But other dances are for everyone. Listen to the emcee—when he announces an "inter-tribal dance," that means everyone, Indian and non-Indian alike, can join in. Kids who aren't inhibited will love going around the circle with the dancers.

Because the drums used at powwows are considered sacred, no alcohol is served nor allowed on the grounds during a powwow. But there will be food—and lots of it. Look for traditional Indian specialties such as corn soup and the traditional powwow food—fry-bread tacos.

In a way, fry bread symbols the resilience of the Indian people. Forced onto reservations, far from their traditional gardens and hunting grounds, the Indian people were expected to subsist on a meager ration of lard and white flour. From these unpromising ingredients, Indians created fry bread.

Granted, bread dough fried in lard and topped with meat and cheese might make nutritionists frown, but a fry-bread taco is also crunchy, spicy, and delicious. It's the perfect food for a celebration of survival against great odds. Will the kids like it? Well, tell them it's a chalupa and they'll love it.

FOR MORE INFORMATION

Minocqua-Arbor Vitae-Woodruff Area Chamber of Commerce, 8216 Highway 51N, (715) 356-5266, www.minocqua.org.

Lac du Flambeau Chamber of Commerce, 14075 Gauthier Lane, (715) 588-3346.

THINGS TO SEE AND DO

Bearskin State Trail. Contact Trout Lake Forestry Headquarters, 4125 Highway M, Boulder Junction, (715) 385-2727.

Dr. Kate Museum, 923 2nd Ave., Woodruff. Open 11 a.m. to 4 p.m. mid-May through Labor Day, (715) 356-6896.

George W. Brown Jr. Ojibwa Museum and Cultural Center, Lac du Flambeau, Open Memorial Day to Labor Day, (715) 588-3333.

Wa-Swa-Goning Indian Village, Highway H, Lac du Flambeau. Open Memorial Day through Labor Day, (715) 588-3560.

Lac du Flambeau Powwow information, (715) 588-3333.

PLACES TO STAY

The Pointe, Highway 51, Minocqua, (715) 356-4431.

The Beacons of Minocqua, 8250 Northern Rd., Minocqua, (715) 356-5515.

Northern Highland State Forest, DNR Headquarters, 8770 Highway J, Woodruff, (715) 356-5211. For reservations, call (888) 947-2757 or check the Web site, www.reserveamerica.com.

PLACES FOR FOOD

Bosaki's Boat House, Highway 51, Minocqua, (715) 356-5292.

The Cottage Inn, Bearskin Trail, Hazelhurst, (715) 356-5444.

Hazelhurst Pub & Grub, Bearskin Trail, Hazelhurst, (715) 356-9400.

Island Café, 314 Oneida, Minocqua, (715) 356-6977.

Little Musky Bar, 1455 Highway 51, Arbor Vitae, (715) 356-6738.

Mama's, Highway 70 West, Minocqua, (715) 356-5070.

Pope's Gresham Lodge, AV4042 Pope Rd., Woodruff, (715) 385-2742.

The Rustic Inn, Bearskin Trail, Hazelhurst, (715) 356-6996.

Nicolet National Forest and Eagle River

After a few days of camping in the North Woods, our eyes, tortured by daily fluorescent lights and television screens, begin to relax in the yellow-green forest light that evolution intended for them. Light in the massive forest of northeastern Wisconsin filters through a thick canopy of sugar maple, birch, and beech leaves before it reaches the ground.

Nicolet National Forest

A great place to experience that light and spend a couple of hours with children contemplating the peacefulness of nature is on the Franklin-Butternut nature trail, located in the Nicolet National Forest about 15 miles east of Eagle River. The 1-mile trail begins in the Franklin Lake campground and winds toward Butternut Lake. You can pause to check for bear paw prints in the sand at Butternut Lake and worship in the church of nature in the Hemlock Cathedral, where ancient hemlock and 400-year-old pines soar to the sky. The trail packs a lot of north for the punch—beyond the lake shore and forest, it travels over a boardwalk through a bog, giving children a close-up look at a floating ecosystem.

The campgrounds in the Eagle River district of Nicolet may provide the best value for a family vacation in the area. The problem may be choosing your campground. Each of the nine campgrounds has its devotees, but the three most popular are probably Spectacle Lake, Luna-White Deer Lakes, and Franklin Lake. Each campground has its charms, and you can broaden your vacation by bringing bikes and making day trips to a different beach each day. (Even the lakes without actual beaches make interesting destinations. Try to visit Four Johns Lake, Three Ducks Lake, and One Wolf Lake just for the fun of it.) Children we know once spent a happy afternoon catching troublesome black flies and feeding them to the carnivorous sundew flowers growing on a lake-edge bog at one of these tiny lakes.

The lake resorts around Eagle River are great places for family reunions and for patriotic parades on the Fourth of July.

Spectacle Lake, shaped like a pair of eyeglasses, is a favorite with families and features a beach and lakefront camping. To reach Spectacle Lake from Eagle River, take Highway 70 east about 7 miles, then left (north) on Military Road, also known as Forest Road 2178. From there, it's another 6 or so miles to Spectacle Lake, via Anvil Lake Road (Forest Road 2465) and Kentuck Lake Road. (Here's an interesting side story to tell kids: the Kentuck Lake area was settled about a century ago by settlers who had their roots in the hills of Kentucky, and some of their traditions and pronunciations still persist today.)

Other campers swear by the campground that occupies the isthmus between Luna and White Deer Lakes—two undeveloped jewels set deep within the forest. Instead of turning left at Military Road, turn right (south) instead. Turn left at Butternut Road (Forest Road 2181) and right again at the Crossover Road (past Eagle River Nordic, an excellent winter destination for cross-country skiers). Turn left again at Four Ducks Road and look for campground signs.

White Deer features a fabulous sandy beach with regular children's nature programs (including printing T-shirts with frozen fish stamps) and a nice 2-mile trail that hugs the lake and is easy for kids to manage. Loons are common summer residents.

Franklin Lake (Military Road to Butternut Lake Road) has the largest campground and the widest offerings, including a small nature museum and trailheads that lead deeper into the forest. At the far end of the campground, you'll find a half-mile trail that leads to tiny Sunfish Lake, the kind of place that makes you feel like you just discovered it. You can spend hours catching and corralling the tiny frogs that hatch in puddles along the lakeshore.

Many experienced Franklin Lake campers bring their boats and request the sites on the high, piney ridge at the far end of the campground—a good place to hear the caroling of the loons and see the bald eagles soaring overhead. In the late 1990s, a bald eagle made its nest just west of the beach. Kids could find fish bones left over from baby eagle meals scattered around the bottom of the tree and the occasional eagle feather. (You can't keep them, though, or you'll violate federal wildlife laws.)

Nicolet campers always bring plenty of bug spray, because the area has numerous low spots for breeding bugs. And don't forget to pack bikes and beach toys.

At night, when the fire is burning low and the loons are raising their wild howls out on the lake, it's time to tell the story of the Hodag. In our version, the mythical beast of the North Woods has burning red eyes, the head of an ox, the feet of a bear, the back of a Stegosaurus, and the tail of an alligator. He terrified the loggers of the North Woods and, if you tell the story right, he'll scare your kids too. On the way home, take the skeptical ones to the park in Rhinelander where there's a statue of the Hodag. You can buy Hodag postcards and souvenirs in Rhinelander as well.

Back to Civilization—Eagle River

Of course, even the most forest-loving folks have to go into town now and again. Eagle River looks like the center of civilization after you've been in the woods for awhile. Children love nothing better than prowling the souvenir shops on the main drag, looking for the perfect piece of ticky-tacky to remember their vacation. Kids can literally spend hours at places like the Moccasin Shop or the Ben Franklin looking for a plastic tomahawk or a postcard showing a walleye the size of a cow.

On rainy afternoons, downtown Eagle River can resemble Times Square, as the summer residents of dozens of area lakes descend upon Wall Street looking for a cure for cabin fever. Fortunately, the Vilas Cinema generally shows matinees of family movies on rainy summer days and the much-beloved popcorn wagon provides a snack to give you strength for your shopping.

Even more fortunately, the Northwoods Children's Museum opened in 1998, giving parents and children a much-needed break when the weather is not so great for the great outdoors. Children can play "up north" in a pioneer cabin, cooking lunch on a replica wood stove and eating at a rustic table. There's a fire tower and ranger station where kids can learn to spot fire and identify trees. The fishing pond is an especially nice touch for kids whose parents are cursed when it comes to catching the real thing.

Fun Up North

Across
2. A fighting fish.
3. In winter on snow, in summer on water.
4. What you do in a tent
Down
1. A colorful pan fish.
3. One way to get wet.
4. A northern home.

(Solution on page 142)

The museum is located at 346 W. Division Street, north and west of the downtown. Take Willow Street, north of Highways 17–70, a block or so west of McDonalds. (Look for the pink and yellow museum signs.)

Kids also enjoy poking around the Vilas County Historical Museum in Sayner (although it's definitely not a hands-on place). They'll see an entire zoo's worth of stuffed animals, items from the pioneer days, and (Tada!!) the world's first snowmobile. Sayner general store owner Carl Eliason invented his "motorboggan" back in 1924, and the Eliason name is still prominent in the area. Sayner is about 15 miles from Eagle River; take Highway 70 west to St. Germain, then Highway 155 north.

Some Area Eateries

In the area, a favorite restaurant is the Clear View Supper Club—a log cabin restaurant dating back to the 1920s, located on the north shore of Big St. Germain. It's rustic, kid-friendly, and has a beach with swing sets where kids can wear off some energy before dinner.

Because it's a vacation area, most of the restaurants in the North are casual and kid-friendly. Some of our favorites near the Nicolet Forest campgrounds include Captain Nemo's, located on Highway 70 near the turn off for the Nicolet forest (kids like its tanks of live fish), and The Chanticleer, which offers excellent food in a pretty setting on Dollar Lake.

We also like Eagle Waters Resort, an old-fashioned family style resort with a dining room open to the public. Years ago, Eagle Waters was one of the few resorts open to Jewish people when many of the locals advertised their bigotry with signs that read "selected clientele only." Kids enjoy playing on the swings and eating the Mickey Mouse sundaes, that have cookies for mouse ears.

For a small town cafe feel, try the Colonial House Restaurant in Eagle River which has neat photos of Eagle River history. In Three Lakes, visit Kristine's Restaurant, a small homey place with great chili and hearty breakfasts.

Biking and Canoeing

Even if you didn't bring your own bikes, you can still book a bicycle trip from Great Northern Adventure Company in Eagle River. The group offers guided four-hour tours through the forest. The routes pass the Wisconsin River and include a lakeside lunch.

If you've ever looked longingly at the fast-moving, boulder-strewn stretch of the Wisconsin River just west of Eagle River, you can outfit yourself for a tubing or canoeing trip there. Hawk's Nest Eagle River Canoe & Tubing, located right on the river, can rent you equipment and pick you up at the end of the trip.

History and Geography Lessons

If you're one of those parents who can't let a vacation pass without slipping in a bit of education with the sand castle building and worm drowning, the Nicolet Forest has those opportunities too.

If you head 50 miles southeast of Eagle River to Laona (which is still in the middle of the vast forest), you can put children in touch with Wisconsin's lumberjack history at the Camp Five Logging Museum. The visit begins with a ride on the "Lumberjack Special" steam train, sure to please both the little kids and big little kids in your family. From Eagle River, take Highway 45 south to Three Lakes, then Highway 32 south to Laona.

Head north if you want to teach geography. Lac Vieux Desert is the large lake on the Michigan border where the Wisconsin River begins. The name comes from ancient gardens discovered on islands inhabited by the Ojibwa Indians, and means, roughly, old civilization. Kids from southern Wisconsin, who know the river as the mammoth waterway that empties into the Mississippi at Wyalusing, get a kick out of seeing it in its infancy. It

Whether you're fishing, canoeing, or tubing, all the lakes of the Nicolet National Forest make you want to take to the water.

flows out of Lac Vieux Desert as a knee-deep stream, so narrow you can nearly jump across. Tell your kids they can brag they threw a ball all the way across the Wisconsin River.

Another geography lesson can be had farther to the west, where Highway B heads from Land O' Lakes to Presque Isle. The road roughly follows the continental divide, crossing it between High and Devils lakes. Tell the kids that a raindrop falling on the south side of the road will flow into the Wisconsin River and end up in the Mississippi and, ultimately, the Gulf of Mexico. Water falling on the north side will end up flowing into Lake Superior, then through the Great Lakes and out the St. Lawrence River to the North Atlantic Ocean.

It's a lesson that makes the North Woods, which can seem like the middle of nowhere, feel like the center of the world.

FOR MORE INFORMATION
Eagle River Chamber of Commerce, 116 S. Railroad St., (800) 359-6315.

THINGS TO SEE AND DO
Great Northern Adventure, P.O. Box 961, Eagle River, (715) 479-8784.
Hawk's Nest Eagle River Canoe & Tubing, Highway 70 West, Eagle River, (715) 479-7944.
Northwoods Children's Museum, 346 W. Division St., Eagle River, (715) 479-4623.

Vilas Cinema, 216 E. Wall St., Eagle River, (715) 479-6541.
Vilas County Historical Museum, 217 Main St., Sayner, (715) 542-3388.

PLACES TO STAY

Chanticleer, 1458 E. Dollar Lake Rd., Eagle River, (715) 479-4486.
Eagle Waters Resort, 3958 Eagle Waters Rd., Eagle River, (715) 479-4411.
Nicolet National Forest, Eagle River Ranger Station, (715) 479-2827.
  To reserve campsites, call (877) 444-6777.

PLACES FOR FOOD

Captain Nemo's 3310 Highway 70 East, Eagle River, (715) 479-2250.
Clear View Supper Club, 8599 N. Big St. Germain Lake Rd., St. Germain, (715) 542-3474.
Colonial House, 125 S. Railroad St., Eagle River, (715) 479-9424.
Kristine's, 1802 Superior St., Three Lakes, (715) 546-3030.

Waupaca and Appleton

If there's one thing the weekend tours in this book offer, it's variety, and this one is no exception. From a watery adventure, to a sobering bit of history, to shopping malls, and more, this tour has something for even the most hard-to-please family members.

Crystal River Canoeing

There's something fun about taking your children on an adventure that you took as a child—and finding that it hasn't changed much at all.

This may happen on a canoe trip on the Crystal River. A good place to begin your adventure is at Ding's Dock, located on Columbia Lake along Highway Q, about 6 miles southwest of Waupaca. The dock is adjacent to the Indian Crossing Casino, an old-fashioned dance hall that offers an array of big name dance bands all summer long. The dock looks much as it did when it first started ferrying tourists on canoe trips back in the 1950s.

To a baby boomer who first experienced the Crystal River in the 1960s, all the important details remain. The water flowing out of the Chain O' Lakes is still crystal clear, the ride is still just scary enough to be fun, and the tippy, little canoes still leave pesky fiberglass fibers in your legs.

The pair of eight-year-old girls on our trip looked a bit worried as the large boat towing the canoes left the dock. After all, it was painted with a toothy grin that looked like a snarling shark.

After a 20-minute cruise on part of the Chain O' Lakes, the boat let us out where the Crystal River empties out of Long Lake. We waded in knee-deep water to our two-person canoes. We soon learned why the operators are adamant about not bringing anything along—even experienced canoeists will tip these bobbing boats a few times on the trip. But, that's part of the fun.

The three-hour trip takes you through forests, a large wetland area, and past numerous cottages. We realized we weren't only being entertained—we were part of the entertainment for the locals who set up lawn chairs to watch the river at rapids and other spots where we would be likely to dump.

Don't be scared, the boat that ferries families from Ding's Dock to the beginning of the Crystal River Canoe Trips only looks like it might bite. Your biggest danger is that you're definitely going to get wet along the way.

Be sure to tuck a few quarters in a deep pocket. When you go through the picture-book village of Rural, you'll go under a bridge and get out of your canoe for the only portage of the trip. If you cross the side road to the Rural Store, you'll find a country store where hand-dipped ice cream cones are just a quarter. At the end of your journey, you'll wait for the bus back to the landing at a well-marked parking spot.

Our advice for the trip is to pick a warm day because you'll be wet most of the time, wear light pants to protect your legs from the fiberglass, and bring lots of sun block. The water is generally less than three feet deep, but the trip isn't recommended for children younger than six because of the frequent spills.

Post-Canoeing Activities

Once you're out of the canoe, treat yourself to a summer meal. There are many nice spots around the lakes. One of our favorites is Clear Water Harbor, located on Taylor Lake, at the northeast end of the Chain O' Lakes near the Wisconsin Veterans Home in King. If it's a nice day, ask to dine on the outside patio for a little bit of Key West in Wisconsin. It features a pier, an outdoor bar, and umbrellas for shade. There are often beach volleyball games in the water and kids can goof around on the pier while they wait for lunch.

Clear Water Harbor is also where you catch the Lady of the Lakes or the Chief Waupaca, sternwheelers that give tours of the lakes. The boats feature regular cruises during the summer months, and on Sundays there is a brunch cruise at 10:30 A.M.

Just up Highway QQ, you'll see the Wisconsin Veterans Home at King. The bulk of today's 700 residents are from the World War II generation. The grounds, which frequently feature events such as Civil War encampments, are open to the public. The home began as the Grand Army of the Republic Home, admitting its first resident, a Civil War widow, in 1887.

King is a good place to talk with children about the sacrifices veterans made for our country. Across the road, you'll see the veterans' cemetery, with its rows of identical stones. If you drive into the cemetery and keep to the right, part way up the hill, you'll come to a lone grave in a small triangle of grass. It is the resting place of "Brownie," a dog that served in World War II. Although the dog died in 1949, his grave is always decorated with flags and flowers.

Brownie, who was born in King, entered the K-9 corps and served overseas. He received an eye injury in 1944 and was sent home. Brownie became the mascot of the human veterans at King and was a familiar sight, begging for treats, until he was killed by a hit-and-run driver in 1949. He was buried with full military honors in the veterans' cemetery.

Camping and Other Fun in Waupaca

There are plenty of places to stay in the Waupaca/Chain O' Lakes area, from resorts to motels to campgrounds. Hartman Creek State Park is on the western edge of the chain and contains several of the chain lakes within its boundaries. It features pine forest campgrounds, a good swimming lake, and a nice picnic area in a separate part of the park, known as the Whispering Pines.

Another favorite campground lies about 10 miles east of Waupaca, near Fremont. Backpacking purists might cringe, but families with young children swear by the Yogi Bear Jellystone Park Camp Resort on Partridge Lake. (In fact, sometimes they swear about it, because once their children stay there, they refuse to vacation anywhere else.)

The park, which won a national award in 1998, is located on Partridge Lake, a wide area in the famed Wolf River. There's great fishing nearby, and for little kids, the park offers all the usual resort amenities: a heated pool, mini golf, a store, an arcade, and a full day of children's activities. Look for the free water-ski shows on the Wolf River on Wednesday and Sunday evenings.

Waupaca's Water Thrills Park is a miniature version of Wisconsin Dells, with waterslides, go-karts, mini golf and an area for paintball wars. If it rains, the Waupaca Bowl and Central Lanes, both in Waupaca, have bowling and there's a four-screen theater, the Rosa, on Main Street in Waupaca.

Appleton—Museums and Malls

If it looks like a long patch of rainy weather, you might want to drive 30 miles east on Highway 10 to Appleton. When combined, the communities in the Fox Cities area form what could be Wisconsin's second largest city and offer plenty family activities.

Little kids and those up through late elementary school will like the Fox Cities Children's Museum, which features lots of hands-on gizmos, including a display opened in 2000 that puts kids at the controls of a space ship. There's also a giant human heart (made by the F.A.S.T. Corporation, mentioned in the Elroy-Sparta bike trail chapter). Kids learn how blood moves through the body by sliding through the anatomically correct organ. The museum is located in the Avenue Mall downtown, at 100 W. College Avenue.

When you're downtown, you might want to check out the display on Appleton's slipperiest son, Harry Houdini, at the Houdini Historical Center, 330 E. College Avenue. After checking out the handcuffs and other paraphernalia of the escape artist, you can take a walking tour of downtown Appleton that takes in several sites important to Houdini, includ-

Every child can be "Queen for a Day" in the dress-up room at the Fox Cities Children's Museum in Appleton.

ing the Lawe Street bridge over the Fox River. This is where Houdini fell in as a youth—the incident that allegedly created his "deep seated need to escape."

If you have adolescents along, they'll undoubtedly be ready to escape all this education. Take them to the Fox River Mall, one of the best in the state. Why do we like it better than the big city malls? Well, in addition to the usual anchor department stores, it has a Target right in the mall. There's also a 10-screen movie theater and the Fox River Brewing Co., where poor mom and dad can sip micro-brewed beer and eat deep-fried lake perch while the teens shop. Kids will like the wide selection at the food court. (Our favorite teen meal: homemade fries from the Steak Escape accompanied by a huge wedge of pizza from Sbarro.)

In addition to the usual mall sprawl, you'll find some interesting spots located in the blocks around the mall, including Funset Boulevard, an indoor sports palace, with virtual reality, video games, laser tag, and indoor golf.

Vande Walle's Candies, located on Mall Drive, is a hometown candy company started by some of the Dutch immigrants who settled this area. You can tour the small factory and watch candy being made. But beware, you won't be able to leave without a box or two.

Nearby is a great hometown-secret spot for value-minded (also known as cheap) parents—the Jansport outlet store. You'll find it in the Jansport factory about a mile west of the mall, at the intersection of Highway 96 and Highway CB. Jansport prints university and other logos on very high quality T-shirts and other sports apparel. The outlet store has the mistakes and overstocked items. Where's Tieko Post University? Who cares, when a heavy pullover sweatshirt with that logo is just $8? You can find great discounts on backpacks and other kiddie wear.

Before heading back to the campground, don't forget to stock up on $5 T-shirts for the whole family to replace those that were soaked in the Crystal River.

FOR MORE INFORMATION

Fox Cities Convention and Visitors Bureau, 3433 College Ave., Appleton, (920) 734-3358 or (800) 2DO-MORE, www.foxcities.com.
Waupaca Area Chamber of Commerce, 221 S. Main St., (715) 258-7343 or (888) 417-4040, www.waupacaareachamber.com.

THINGS TO SEE AND DO

Ding's Dock (for Crystal River canoe trips), N 2498 W. Columbia Lake Dr., Waupaca, (715) 258-2612. Generally open early May to September.
Central Lanes, 408 Oak St., Waupaca, (715) 258-2622.
Clear Water Harbor, N 2757 Highway QQ, Waupaca. (715) 258-2866 for information on Chief Waupaca and Lady of the Lakes cruises.
Fox Cities Children's Museum, 100 W. College Ave., Appleton, (920) 734-3226, www.funatfccm.org.
Fox River Mall, College Ave. at Highway 41, Appleton, (920) 739-4100.
Funset Boulevard, 3916 W. College Ave., Appleton, (920) 993-0909.
Houdini Historical Center (part of the Outagamie County Historical Museum), 330 E. College Ave., Appleton, (920) 733-8445.
Indian Crossing Casino (food and dancing), 1171 Highway Q, Waupaca, (715) 258-3332.
Jansport Outlet Store, Highways 96 and CB, Appleton, (920) 734-9812.
Rosa Theater, 218 S. Main St., Waupaca, (715) 258-2510.
Vande Walle's Candies, 400 Mall Dr., Appleton, (920) 738-7799.

Waupaca Bowl Bowling Lane, 810 Bowling Lane, Waupaca, (715) 258-8915.
Waupaca Water Thrills Park, 711 Shadow Rd., Waupaca, (715) 258-8122.

PLACES TO STAY

Hartman Creek State Park, N 2480 Hartman Creek Rd., Waupaca,
   (715) 258-2372.
Yogi Bear Jellystone Camp Resort, E 6506 Highway 10/110, Fremont,
   (800) 258-3315, www.yogifremont.com.

PLACES FOR FOOD

Clear Water Harbor, N 2757 Highway QQ, Waupaca, (715) 258-9912 for the
   restaurant and bar.

The Wausau Area

It could happen to you. You're southbound on Interstate 39, after a long and expensive ski trip to the Upper Peninsula of Michigan. It's snowing hard, traffic is Sunday-night heavy, and you're not even half way home. Suddenly, a good-sized ski hill looms into view, with its long white runs glistening under the lights, while skiers the size of ants make looping turns.

"Hey," says a cranky child's voice from the back of the van. "Why couldn't we just ski there?"

Skiing at Rib Mountain

Why not, indeed. Rib Mountain and the other winter sports venues in the Wausau area play host to more than 6,000 skiers, snowboarders, skaters, and other winter sports nuts for the Badger State Winter Games. On other weekends it hosts hockey tournaments and ski races.

The Rib Mountain Ski Area has 12 runs ranging from bunny to advanced, three lifts, and boasts a 624-foot vertical drop, by far the biggest in the state. It also has cheaper rates than the bigger hills to the south and north (just $10 a ticket on weekdays). If you think the lighted hill looks nice from the highway, wait until you see the lights of Wausau from the hill.

Rib Mountain has two kinds of ski runs: at the bottom you'll find wide, gently sloping trails for beginners; at the top, there are steep intermediate and advanced hills with moguls. The rental set-up, however, needs a bit of polish. Although the staff is friendly and helpful, the equipment is worn and the layout requires you to try on the boots in a separate building, making for a long clomp back to the rental shed if the boots don't fit.

You'll like the chalet, a roomy building with plenty of booths and a nice view of the hill. A family of four can dine on a kid-friendly menu of hotdogs, pizza, grilled cheese, and the like for under $20.

My only criteria for a ski-trip hotel is that it have an indoor pool and whirlpool to soak away the soreness. The Rib Mountain Inn, with its ski hill location, lacks a general pool, but does have some fireside villas that include whirlpools, as well as kitchens (which can make the family ski trip a lot easier

Are We Up North Yet?

Your parents load you in the car and tell you that you're going "Up North." But, where, exactly, is Up North??

If you're from Illinois, you might already be Up North, because many people barely cross the state line to vacation in the lake area near Lake Geneva and Delavan.

If you believe the signs, Portage, about 70 miles north of the Illinois border, claims to be "Where the North begins." By the way, *portage* is French for carrying a canoe on the back. That's what Indians and explorers did at Portage, where the Wisconsin River (which flows south into the Mississippi River) and the Fox River (which flows north into the Great Lakes) come within a mile of each other.

If you'd rather trust science, ecologists say there's a zone running through the mid-section of Wisconsin called "the Tension Zone." It's where the trees and animals of the south end and the trees and animals of the north begin. You're traveling through the tension zone when you start seeing fewer maple trees and more pines. Lots of places advertise being "North of the Tension Zone," but it doesn't really mean your parents will be less crabby.

If you want to trust the map, you're definitely Up North when you cross the 45th parallel. It's a line on your map that runs from Hudson on the border of Minnesota to Jacksonport on the Lake Michigan shore. It marks the halfway line between the equator and the North Pole.

Depending on where your family likes to vacation, your Up North might be the Wisconsin Dells, Door County, Hayward, or the Chequamegon Bay. It could be the popular fishing lakes up around Crandon or farther north, near Minocqua and Three Lakes. Or, it could be on the Waupaca Chain O' Lakes or in the woods near Black River Falls.

Wherever it is, you'll know you're there when you see log cabins and pine trees. That's when you'll be north of the Tension Zone for sure.

on the wallet). Wausau also has a host of hotel chains and locally owned hotels with the requisite pools and spas.

If folks in your group are hankering for a change of pace, and there's a model railroad buff among them, check out the Hobby Connection, located in Rothschild on Highway 51 South across from the Weyerhauser plant. On Saturdays, the Hobby Connection opens its basement to the public; you'll find a huge model railroad set-up that depicts the actual rail lines between Wausau and Stevens Point. Kids can walk through the giant double helix of connecting rail lines.

Other Skiing in the Area

Rib Mountain isn't the only ski hill in this sports-mad town. Across the Wisconsin River and up the hills on the east side of town, you'll find Sylvan Hill, a ski and sled hill run by the Marathon and Wausau parks departments. The hill, with its four tow ropes, is perfect for beginning and intermediate skiers. Even better are the lift tickets, which cost $4 for a child's full day ticket and $6 for an adult. Rentals are available at a very reasonable fee.

On four Saturdays every January, the park hosts "Ski for Youth," which offers free skiing, half price rentals, free lessons, and races for children 17 and younger. If your kids think the hill sounds too wimpy, tell them this is where the Badger State Games holds its Quadrathlon, a grueling event that combines winter running with races on cross-country skis, snow shoes,

Winter doesn't hinder the fun in the sports-mad city of Wausau, where the parks feature sledding, skiing, and other snow fun.

and mountain bikes. There are cross-country trails at Sylvan, as well. To find Sylvan, take Sixth Street north from downtown Wausau, turn right at Horseshoe Springs Road, and right again at Sylvan Street.

Besides a sledding hill near Sylvan, there are city owned hills at Schofield Park, 606 E. Randolph Street, Riverside Park, 100 Sherman Street, and 3M Park, 405 Park Boulevard. The sledding hill at Pleasant View Park, 1221 Sumner Street, has lights for night sledding.

The area's premier Nordic ski area is the Nine Mile Forest, located south of Rib Mountain. The area hosts the Badger State Games and Snekkevik Classic each year, and also has a chalet with rental skis, lessons, and a Nordic Ski Patrol.

The area requires a daily trail pass, but the nominal fee ($4 for an adult with a child of 12 or younger) is worth it. The 20 miles of wooded trails are groomed regularly, with a wide skating lane and tracks for diagonal skiers. There's even a short kids' loop for children who are just trying out the sport.

To find it, take exit 188 off I-39, go west 3.5 miles on Highway N, then turn south (left) on Red Bud Road.

A Museum Kids Will Like

Of course, the other advantage of taking a Wausau ski weekend is that after you get off the slopes, there are plenty of things to do.

Take culture, for example. Even parents who normally cringe at the thought of taking their brood to an art museum should consider the Leigh Yawkey Woodson Art Museum. Admission is free and they welcome children, going to the extreme of sponsoring Toddler Tuesdays for that most rambunctious age group of them all. Besides, kids like the idea of going to a former mansion. It's located in the Andrew Warren historic district just east of downtown—a 10-block area full of fabulous restored homes from the lumber baron era.

The museum's sculpture garden is a nice place to wander. Some of the pieces are whimsically appealing to children: a giant pink rabbit's foot hanging from a tree, a hippo partly hidden in the snow, and a horse that looks like it's made of driftwood but is actually bronze.

When the museum has displays that have kid appeal, it opens its family exploration gallery to showcase related ideas. For example, when the museum held an exhibit of Australian Aboriginal Art called "Bushfire," the family gallery had displays of stuffed koala bears for kids to play with and a giant felt board where they could create their own aboriginal style art.

The museum seems to have a knack for finding exhibits that, though artistically meritorious, appeal to a broad range of people, children included. One recent exhibit on Children's Book Illustrations included story hours for children and illustrations from a wide variety of children's books. Related activities brought in illustrators from around the globe, and included book making workshops, tea parties, and other fun events.

The museum also had exhibits of sports figures as depicted in art, teapots, and nature art. It is probably best known for its annual show, Birds in Art, which draws an international selection of artists who use birds in their work. Birds in Art always has family and children's related events.

Wausau's Diverse Downtown

Speaking of culture, you might be lucky enough to be in town when the Grand Theater, on Fourth Street, is hosting one of its touring or local shows. Recent performances have included such kid-friendly shows as Peter and the Wolf, Children of Eden, and Charley's Aunt. The theater itself is worth a

Not many museums let kids crawl all over their exhibits. But the Leigh Yawkey Woodson Art Museum will. Youngsters (and even adults) can get up close and personal with the artwork in the outdoor sculpture gallery, including this bronze hippo, aptly named *The Heavyweight*. (Photo courtesy of the Leigh Yawkey Woodson Art Museum /© Don Frisque.)

visit—it dates back to 1827 and its glorious marble statuary and colonnades were recently restored.

Of course, there's culture, and there's teen culture. We'd be remiss to those visitors if we didn't point out that downtown Wausau is home to one of central Wisconsin's largest shopping malls. You'll find 66 stores in the shopping center, including anchor department stores. But what's especially nice is the restored downtown pedestrian mall along Third Street. Look for the specialty shops in the Washington Square building. Adults can get their caffeine fix at Something's Brewing, while kids can get candy and ice cream cones topped with sprinkles at the soda fountain at Michael's Candies.

Another block down Third Street, you'll see the Back When Cafe which has historical decor and great homemade pies and soups. At night, it features live jazz and a gourmet menu, but at lunch it's a fine place to take kids.

Another good place to dine in downtown Wausau is the Peking restaurant, located in the Landmark Building (the former Hotel Wausau) on Scott Street. You dine in the faded elegance of the old ballroom on Chinese food ranging from sweet and sour dishes that kids like to more adventurous fare.

One of the best places to unwind after a day on the ski slopes has to be Mino's, an Italian Supper Club located north of downtown Wausau at Sixth Street and Golf Course Road. It's a family-friendly place with excellent food. Dinners begin with chewy Italian bread, baked on a stone and brought hot from the oven. There's an excellent spiced olive oil for dipping, but the waitress will also bring butter for the kids.

The menu includes such Italian cuisine as calamari soup, an excellent concoction of squid, and pasta in a deeply flavored Italian broth. The penne alla vodka, in a sweet tomato cream sauce, was as subtle as the pasta e fasuli (a Sicilian dish of pasta with onion and 15 kinds of beans) was hearty and earthy.

If this sounds like stuff your children would never, ever touch, don't worry. Mino's has an extensive pasta menu ranging from spaghetti with meatballs or meat sauce to lasagna to cheese tortellini. And don't forget the excellent homemade pizzas (also baked to crunchy goodness on the pizza stone). They're good enough to order an extra one to take back to the hotel for midnight snacks.

Poniatowski— The Center of the World

For an educational side trip, chuck the kids in the car and go about 15 miles north and west of Wausau. When the kids ask where you're going, tell them you're headed to the center of the world.

Actually, Poniatowski is the center of the northern half of the Western Hemisphere (or the western half of the Northern Hemisphere.)

In a cornfield just outside of town is the spot where the 45th parallel crosses the principal meridian. This means Poniatowski is not only halfway between the North Pole and the equator but exactly one quarter of the way around the globe from the prime meridian, which runs through the Royal Observatory in Greenwich, England.

There are eight spots like this on Earth—where the 45th parallels north and south cross the four longitudinal lines that divide the Earth like a quartered orange. Five of them are under the oceans. The other two are near Bordeaux, France, and near the border of northwestern China and Mongolia.

You're now nearly a member of the Poniatowski 45 × 90 Club. Started by the late John Gesicki, who ran the local general store, the only membership requirement is that you visit the spot where the 45th crosses the 90th meridian and sign the log book. At last count, there were more than 6,000 signatures, from as far away as China, Africa, and Italy. John's widow, Lorretta, still keeps the book at the store and tavern, across from the Catholic Church in Poniatowski. You can also pick up nifty 45 × 90 Club bumper stickers that proclaim you've visited Poniatowski.

To find Poniatowski, take Highway 29 west from Wausau about 11 miles, turn right (north) on Highway H, go 2 miles and turn left on Highway U.

Now you've learned two important lessons about Wisconsin geography on this trip: we are the center of the world, and it's a lot easier to take ski trips closer to home. Maybe that kid in the backseat was actually reading a map.

FOR MORE INFORMATION
Wausau Convention & Visitors Bureau, 10204 Park Plaza, Suite B, Mosinee, (888) 948-4748.

THINGS TO SEE AND DO
Gesicki Store, Highway U, Poniatowski, (715) 352-3094.

Grand Theater, 415 4th St., Wausau, (715) 842-0988.

The Hobby Connection, 503 S. Grand Ave. (Business 51), Rothschild, (715) 355-4100.

Leigh Yawkey Woodson Museum, 700 N. 12th St., Wausau, (715) 845-7010, Tuesday– Friday, 9 A.M.–4 P.M.; Saturday–Sunday, noon–5 P.M.; closed Mondays and holidays.

Nine Mile Forest, Red Bud Rd., (715) 261-1580.

Rib Mountain (skiing), Park Rd., (715) 845-2846.

Sylvan Hill (skiing), Sylvan St., (715) 842-5411; Wausau Parks Department, (715) 261-1550.

PLACES TO STAY
Ameri-Host Inn, 400 Orbiting Dr., Mosinee, (715) 693-9000.

Baymont Inn, 1910 Stewart Ave., Wausau, (715) 842-0421; (800) 301-0200.

Country Inns and Suites, 1520 Metro Dr., Schofield, (715) 359-1881; (800) 456-4000.

Hampton Inn, 615 S. 24th Ave., Wausau, (715) 848-9700.

Ramada Inn, 201 N. 17th Ave., Wausau, (715) 845-4341; (800) 754-9728.

Rib Mountain Inn, 2900 Rib Mountain Way, Wausau, (715) 848-2802.

PLACES FOR FOOD
Back When Café, 606 3rd St., Wausau, (715) 848-5668.

Michael's Candies, 300 3rd St., Wausau, (715) 842-7222.

Mino's, 900 Golf Course Rd., Wausau, (715) 675-5939.

Peking, 221 Scott St., Wausau, (715) 842-8080.

section 2
The Southeast

Lake Geneva

You can just tell that kids are going to like certain things about Wisconsin's oldest resort. They'll like the beaches, the fudge shops, the arcades, and the boats. What we didn't expect is the obsession they developed with the wealthy.

"Holy Moley, look at that one," they hollered, pointing at the huge estates as we drove Wrigley Drive along the lake.

"Yeah," said the older kid, "and that's just the guard house."

There's a reason Lake Geneva was once known as the "Newport of the West." Back in the late nineteenth century, Chicago's wealthy began to build huge estate homes around the lake as their "summer cottages." The trend accelerated following the Chicago fire of 1871, when many of Chicago's elite moved to their summer homes while their main residences were being rebuilt. It reached its peak during the gilded age of 1890 to 1920.

A Cruise on the Lake

Although many of the estates have since been subdivided, you still get a sense of grandeur. However, you can't see most of the big homes from the road. You'll either have to hike the 21-mile path around the lake or get out on the water.

Cruises leave all day long from Riviera Docks in downtown Lake Geneva. The Geneva Lake Cruise Line offers a range of narrated cruises around the lake, ranging from a one-hour ride to an ice cream social tour to an elaborate Sunday brunch cruise. The most unusual trip—and probably the most entertaining for kids—is the two-hour mail boat cruise.

Since 1916, mail boats have delivered the mail to the estates along the lake during what the wealthy call "the season" (and what the rest of us call the summer). Back in the olden days, the swamps around the lake made it difficult to deliver the mail to the lake estates, most of which are located far from the road, and so mail delivery to the docks was born.

As you pass by the many estates, the mail boat captain gives a running commentary on estates with names such as Fairfield, Maple Lawn, Bonnie

49

You can take the mail boat or walk the path to enjoy the Gilded Age splendor along Lake Geneva's shore.

Brae, and Loramor. The kids bored quickly, because the only name they recognized was Wrigley. ("Hey! The guy who invented Juicy Fruit lives there!") But the mail delivery adds extra entertainment value.

The boat never quite stops, as the "mail girl" leaps off, races down the pier, deposits the mail into the box, grabs the mail to be posted, stuffs it in her mouth, and races back to leap aboard. Very rarely the mail deliverers end up in the lake, but the hope that it might happen this time keeps kids entertained.

The other way to see the estates is to hike the 21-mile path that encircles the lake. You can buy the "Walk, Talk, and Gawk" guide at local stores to know what you're gawking at. Older kids might enjoy making the 8-mile hike to Williams Bay. If you stop at the cruise office before you leave, you can make arrangements for the boat to pick you up in Williams Bay and bring you back to Lake Geneva.

Downtown Lake Geneva

Even if you're not planning to cruise, the Riviera Docks in downtown Lake Geneva are a good place to take kids. Here, you can also begin your tour of the city or your walking, skating, or biking tour around the lake. The city bought and renovated the old tile and brick building, which is full of shops offering ice cream, souvenirs, and an arcade. It's a good place to watch boats and people, and to play video games.

Next to the dock is Lake Geneva Beach. Like all the public beaches on the lake—Fontana, Williams Bay, and Big Foot Beach State Park—you must pay if you want to step into the water. The fees are generally $2 to $5 and cover the cost of lifeguards and changing facilities.

Across Wrigley Drive from the Riviera Docks and the beach, you'll find Popeye's restaurant, a good choice for lunch with the kids. Popeye's can be absolutely mobbed in the summer—we've seen the lines snake out into the street—but it has several large dining rooms and can quickly move the people through.

Popeye's is decorated in a nautical theme with dock pilings, old boats, and the like, so even if you didn't get a window table with views of Lake Geneva, you'll still feel like you're on the water. If kids get antsy waiting for a table or food, send them downstairs to Trader Nick's gift shop.

All kids at Popeye's get a children's menu complete with a little sketch pad game that they may keep. With a menu that includes hot dogs, macaroni and cheese, and pizza, and prices that range from $2.97 to $4.47 for a shrimp basket, it's ideal for kids. As for adults, we found that Popeye's "world famous" cheese and broccoli soup could have been used for wallpaper paste but the food was passable and the atmosphere makes it enjoyable.

Kids may enjoy roaming the streets of Lake Geneva. There's an arcade around the corner from Popeye's, on Broad Street. Up on Main Street, you'll find fudge shops, upscale toy shops, such as Alison Wonderland, 720 N. Main Street, souvenir stores, and even a Starbucks. If you have kids who like Chinese food, stop by Temple Garden, which broke the hearts of Madison food lovers by moving to Lake Geneva a few years ago.

A Grand Place to Stay

The area abounds with places to stay, ranging from camping at Big Foot Beach State Park just south of town, to reasonably priced family hotels located along Wells Street (south on Highway H), to posh resorts that would make the industrial barons of nineteenth-century Lake Geneva feel right at home.

We decided to check out the Grand Geneva Resort and Spa, located just east of town near the intersections of Highways 50 and 12. We were partially curious about what had become of the old Playboy Club. (If you think the estates along the lake are part of a different era, try explaining the Playboy Club concept to twenty-first-century kids. "The ladies wore ears and cotton tails? Why?")

Your first clue that the Playboy Club era has passed is the bronze statue next to the parking valets that depicts a laughing child getting a shoulder ride from his dad. The Grand Geneva is now a good place for a family getaway. The Marcus Corporation has invested millions in updating the resort, so that it's very nice, yet still welcoming to families.

The list of resort activities is mind-boggling. In the winter, there's a downhill ski area, cross country trails, and ice skating on the golf course lagoons. In summer, there are two beautiful 18-hole golf courses, tennis courts, and horseback riding at the stables. Year round, guests can use the spa and pools.

There is a kids pool and arcade in the main lodge and a separate lap-pool for those older than 16 in the spa and sports center.

Kids and adults can take trail rides from the Grand Geneva's Dan Patch Stables, located in a white and green farmstead near the entrance to the resort. As much as kids like bobbing along the trails, they enjoy the end of the ride even better, when they may feed corn and hay to the baby goats, llamas, and potbellied pigs on the farm. In the winter, the stable offers sleigh rides and in the summer, carriage rides and "city slicker breakfast rides." There are also a number of other horse stables in the area for kids who like to ride.

Delavan

If you worry that too much lounging around the resort isn't good for kids, Lake Geneva can be a good base for field trips.

Delavan, located about 10 miles west on Highway 50, has a quaint downtown with brick streets. You can learn about the city's nineteenth-century circus legacy and have your photo taken with giant fiberglass statues of an elephant, a clown, and a giraffe. Horton Park, located on Main Street next to the Wisconsin School for the Deaf, has a beach, paths, and a nice picnic area. Because many families of deaf children settle in Delavan to be near the school, you'll see people using American Sign Language all over town. Delavan is also home to a sizable Mexican-American population and has excellent Mexican restaurants, including Hernandez Mexican Food, which combines a restaurant and grocery store.

Yerkes Observatory

On Saturdays, you can attend the free open house between nine A.M. and noon at the Yerkes Observatory located high on a hill in Williams Bay, about 5 miles west of the town of Lake Geneva. Back in the 1880s, astronomers at the University of Chicago needed a place with clear skies not obscured by Chicago's smoke and haze, but with convenient rail connections to the city. They chose the high shore of Lake Geneva, and finished the observatory here in 1897.

Even people who aren't astronomy buffs would be interested in checking out the ornate building. Kids enjoy finding their zodiac signs in the carved pillars out front. Tell them to look for the fat guy who represents a former president of the University of Chicago. There's another guy who looks like Pinocchio with some rough sandstone near his big nose. Guides can show kids how the image once showed the man getting bitten in the nose by a hornet that was supposed to symbolize John D. Rockefeller getting "stung" for more money to build the observatory. Guardians of good taste later ordered the hornets removed.

Many of the exhibits focus on the history of astronomy and the discoveries made here. On Saturday mornings, guides will take you up into the giant dome that houses the largest lens telescope in the world. Kids will get a

The renovated Riviera dock at Lake Geneva is the place to catch cruises on the mail boat and other craft. It's also a great place to buy an ice cream cone or a swimsuit or to fish from the docks out back.

chance to hold a chunk of a 4.5 billion-year-old meteor and a piece of rock from Canada which shows the impression of being smashed by a meteor.

What kids seem to like best about the tour is the optical illusion of sinking when the giant round wooden floor beneath the telescope rises in front of them. There's a small gift shop area where astronomy-related toys and pieces of meteors and tektites are available.

Old World Wisconsin

Another great family field trip, located about a half-hour north of Lake Geneva on Highway 67, is Old World Wisconsin. Run by the State Historical Society, and open during the spring and summer, Old World Wisconsin is a collection of old farmsteads and villages designed to show off Wisconsin's ethnic heritage.

There are German, Norwegian, and Yankee settlements, where kids can walk through the homes and see costumed historical characters feeding the chickens, baking bread, and plowing the fields. The country store is a special favorite, as is the Old World Wisconsin gift shop, where kids can buy penny candy and historically themed items. We especially like the calico poke bonnets for only $6.

There is a lot of walking between farmsteads, so bring strollers or wagons for little kids.

At Old World Wisconsin, the historical interpreters stay in character while they do their presentations. A kid caught chewing gum in the one-room schoolhouse might just have to write on the board for punishment. Kids are

53

free to ask questions and our children—apparently still feeling the effects of those Lake Geneva mansions—grilled the shopkeeper and the shoe maker about their earnings.

"Was this a rich job?" they asked. "How much money did you make? Was that a lot of money back then?"

And we thought vacations weren't educational.

FOR MORE INFORMATION

Lake Geneva Convention & Visitors Bureau, (800) 345-1020,
     www.lakegenevawi.com.

THINGS TO SEE AND DO

Alison Wonderland, 720 N. Main St, Lake Geneva, (262) 248-6500.
Big Foot Beach State Park, 1452 Highway H, Lake Geneva, (262) 248-2528.
Dan Patch Stables, Grand Geneva Resort, (262) 248-3841.
Fantasy Hills Ranch, Highway 67, Delavan, (262) 728-1773.
Fontana Beach, Fontana Blvd., Fontana, (262) 275-6136.
Geneva Lake Cruise Lines (mail boats and other lake tours),
     (800) 558-5911.
Lake Geneva Beach, Wrigley Dr., Lake Geneva, (262) 248-3673.
Lake Geneva Horse and Petting Zoo, Highway 50 at 67, (262) 245-0770.
Old World Wisconsin, S103 W37890 Highway 67, Eagle, (262) 594-6304,
     Fax (262) 594-6342, e-mail: owwvisit@idcnet.com.
Walking Tour of Lake Geneva. The "Walk, Talk & Gawk Guide" is available
     at local stores and by mail, at P.O. Box 689, Williams Bay, WI 53191.
Williams Bay Beach, Geneva St., Williams Bay, (262) 245-2700.
Yerkes Observatory, 373 W. Geneva St., Williams Bay, (262) 245-5555.

PLACES TO STAY

Grand Geneva Resort, Highway 50 at 12, (800) 558-3417,
     www.grandgeneva.com.

PLACES FOR FOOD

Hernandez Mexican Food, 212 Seventh St., Delavan, (262) 728-6443.
Popeye's, 811 Wrigley Dr., (262) 248-4381.
Temple Garden, 724 N. Main St., (262) 249-9188.

Madison

How are you going to decide what to do for a family weekend in Madison? After all, it's the state capital, the site of a major university, Wisconsin's second-largest city, one of the country's best communities for biking, and home to as diverse a populace as you'll ever see. So, let's get our visiting priorities in order.

A Badger Game

There's nothing like an autumn afternoon of college football, and there's no better place to experience it than Madison. If you're taking your child to his or her first Badger game, there should be a few things on your checklist.

Teach your kids the "chicken dance" and the words to "On, Wisconsin," and make sure it's the original football version. (Hint, the second lines should be "plunge right through that line," not the state song version, "grand old Badger State.")

Remember that the wave in "Varsity" begins with your right arm waving to the right.

Get tickets. This is really not as hard as it sounds, despite the fact that Camp Randall is almost always at full capacity. Call the UW ticket office to see if they have tickets available. (The pre-conference season games and the game that falls during deer hunting season generally have plenty available.) Check the want ads in the Madison newspapers, which are also available online at www.madison.com. If all else fails, go about two hours before kick-off and patrol the block of the stadium where you can nearly always find someone selling tickets. The only truly difficult ticket to come by during the Badgers' very successful 1990s was the 1999 game when Heisman Trophy winner Ron Dayne set the NCAA rushing record.

The year before, tickets were going cheap for the Penn State game, when the Badgers clinched a Rose Bowl spot. The reason? That game fell during the Wisconsin high holiday of deer hunting season. There are generally plenty of tickets for the early season games, before the Badgers begin playing their Big Ten schedule.

Once you've got your ticket, your next problem will be finding a place to park. One of the easiest ways for families with children and older adults to get to the stadium is to park in one of the parking ramps surrounding the Capitol Square. For $1 you can park and pick up a shuttle bus that drops you off at Camp Randall. Each additional person is $1 and the ride back to the ramps after the game is free. Buses show up every seven minutes and begin running about three hours before the game.

With a little planning, you can park in the ramp, grab breakfast from one of the Dane County Farmer's Market stalls (more on kids and the market later) and be on your way to the game with the cheapest parking in town.

One reason to get to the game early is to catch the Badger Bash at Union South before the game. The University of Wisconsin Marching Band plays on the terrace between the union and the engineering library an hour before game time. You can grab a brat from the outdoor grill, and if you've forgotten anything important, such as Bucky Badger face tattoos, you can probably purchase it at the gift shop on the ground floor of the union.

Then join the crowd as it escorts the band on a march through the stone archway guarded by the statues of Civil War soldiers. If your kids ask, explain that Camp Randall was the site of a giant civil war camp, and that the soldiers were about the same age as today's football players. That's Old Abe, the Civil War eagle mascot, perched in stone above the gate. He accompanied Wisconsin troops into battle, flying above the fray as they fought.

If the temperature is cool, be sure to bring or buy seat cushions, because those metal benches get mighty chilly. Of course, children's attention tends to wander during the game, so have them watch the cheerleaders and keep an eye out for the wandering tubas (they usually appear toward the end of the third quarter). They also like to watch for the guys without shirts who, strangely enough, grow more numerous as the weather grows colder. One 11-year-old we know fondly calls them "the drunk guys."

This brings to mind some of the things your kids might see and hear. The notoriously rowdy student sections (O and P) have a few regular chants with swear words, and you might encounter a drunk or two. Remember that security is much tighter than during the bench-tossing, body-passing days of the 1980s. If you think someone is out of hand, speak to an usher and he or she will be gone faster than you can say, "Ron Dayne. Run! Run! Run!"

If it's not football season, you may be able to pick up men's and women's basketball tickets from the Kohl Center box office. Both women's volleyball (at the Field House) and basketball (at the Kohl Center) regularly draw thousands of frenzied fans, and feature the band and cheerleaders. Don't underestimate the positive influence that seeing women's sports can have on young girls. As one surprised 6-year-old girl commented excitedly, on attending her first women's basketball game: "All their guys are girls and all our guys are girls, too!"

🌰 Wisconsin Place Names

Can you ride your bike from Rome to London without leaving Wisconsin? Sure you can, and you can stop at the Pyramids on the way. From Rome in eastern Jefferson County you can take town roads north to the Glacial Drumlin State Trail. From there, you can ride east about 20 miles to London, on the Jefferson and Dane county line. Along the way you can stop for a swim at Sandy Beach in Lake Mills. Local lore says there are ancient Indian pyramids located at the bottom of Rock Lake.

What other Wisconsin towns are named for places in other countries? Well, there's Brussels in Door County and Luxemburg to the south in Kewaunee County. Wisconsin has a Berlin and a New Berlin, a Scandinavia, a Stockholm, a Hamburg, a Holland, a Hollandale, a Poland, a Denmark, and a Cuba City. There's New Amsterdam, New Holstein, New Munster, as well as Germania and Polonia. What other ones can you find?

Next, look for names that represent Wisconsin's dairy farming tradition. There's Cream south of Eau Claire and Dairyland south of Superior and Colby near the middle of the state.

You could make a meal out of these Wisconsin towns: Plum City, Sugar Bush, Egg Harbor, Chili, Butternut, and Honey Creek. You could mix them all together in Cooksville.

Besides Porcupine and Elk Mound in western Wisconsin, what other communities are named for animals? Which ones are named for trees?

And what about the names that just sound funny? Make up a story about Luck, Jump River, Humbird, Liberty Pole, Rising Sun, Embarrass, Weyauwega, Wandroos, and Wauwatosa. What would happen if a girl from Angelica married a guy from Goodman at Devils Lake?

Finally, take a color tour of Wisconsin, from Spring Green and Blue Mounds through Black Earth, Brown Deer, Silver Creek, Black River Falls, Whitehall, and Whitelaw. What other colors can you find?

The Farmer's Market

Beyond Badger games, another great Madison institution is the Saturday morning Dane County Farmer's Market, which runs from the last Saturday in April to the first Saturday in November, from 6 A.M. to 2 P.M. Children don't generally have the same interest in ogling organic endive as their parents, but there are plenty of things they will enjoy about the market. Buying straws filled with honey, called "honey sticks," and watching bees work behind glass are favorite activities, as is the live entertainment from the street musicians.

Most kids are happiest when munching donuts and sipping from pint containers of cider. And remember that it's not much fun being a short person in the human gridlock that the market can become. Consider bringing a football or Frisbee and camping out on the Capitol lawn while the other adults in the party navigate the market. (Don't climb the trees, though, because the Capitol police are watching.)

A Capitol Visit and a Trip Down State Street

The Capitol is always worth a visit and not just for the toilets. Kids like to lay on the cool marble floor and stare upward at the painting 200 feet above on the ceiling of the dome. It's called "Resources of Wisconsin," and the sharp-eyed children may be able to pick out the wheat, tobacco, and lead ore in the painting. Free tours of the Capitol leave the information desk in the rotunda on the hour from 9 A.M. to 3 P.M. Ask the guides to show kids the marble steps that contain fossils. On nice days, the Capitol observation deck atop the fourth floor is generally open. Ask a guard for directions if you don't see the signs.

Madison's State Street is home to the Madison Children's Museum, the House of Cheese, and other fun spots for kids to visit.

The State Street corner of the square puts you smack in the middle of Madison's museum row. On your right is the Wisconsin Veteran's Museum, which features fascinating exhibits on wars from the Civil War through the present, and genial veteran tour guides who are excellent at answering children's questions. The State Historical Society Museum, on your left, is full of permanent and changing displays about Wisconsin history, and has a fun gift shop. Most Wisconsin fourth graders visit these museums on school trips, so your children might enjoy showing you around.

A block or so down State Street will take you to the Madison Children's Museum, which is full of attractions for children younger than eight. They can play "Farmer's Market" with a stand full of plastic vegetables, milk a cow, and build with toy cranes. There are regular programs offering the chance to make more elaborate art projects.

A stroll down State Street, with stops at kid-friendly shops such as Puzzle Box and the Game Haven, is also fun for kids. They like the popcorn at Cleary's, near the top of State Street, and ice cream cones from the Chocolate Shoppe, farther down the street.

At the far end of State Street, you'll run into the University of Wisconsin campus, where you'll find Memorial Union at 700 Langdon Street. Having an ice cream cone and a bag of popcorn (shared with the ducks) on the Union Terrace is a time-honored way for Madison kids to spend the afternoon. Memorial Union is also a good starting point for a bike ride along the lakeshore path, which will take you out to Picnic Point and back for a ride that's about 3.5 miles long. Just watch out for the sharp turn onto the point.

Walking and Biking Around Town

Another fun Madison ride, especially for families with older children, is the 5-mile combination of bike paths and streets that circle Lake Monona. In Monona, stop at Winnequah Park to let kids rampage through the incredible wooden play structure. There's also an excellent public pool at Winnequah Park (something the city of Madison lacks) with a waterslide, so bring your suit during swimming season. The Monona Bait & Ice Cream Shop, 4516 Winnequah Road, is a wonderful stop for a hamburger, Babcock Hall ice cream, and worms to go.

Finally, don't forget about the smallest Madison lake, Wingra. You can make an easy trip around the lake, through the Arboretum and onto Monroe Street (where kids should stay on sidewalks and bike paths to avoid traffic). Michael's Frozen Custard, 2531 Monroe Street, makes a mean "hot lava" sundae that includes hot fudge and cherries on custard.

Either begin or end your Lake Wingra tour with a stop at Vilas Zoo, which must certainly be one of the best free zoos in the country. The lion, ape, reptile, and birdhouses have recently been redone, and the children's zoo features petting and feeding. Our favorite is the herpetarium where only thin glass separates you from the alligators. The attached Discovery Center has microscopes and all kinds of neat science activities for kids. The Shriners of Zor Shrine offer camel rides on Sundays. And, there's Vilas Beach across the street for cooling off after a hot tour of the zoo.

Getting Out on the Water

Because Madison is "The City of the Four Lakes," you really should try to get out on the water, if you can. You can rent a canoe or a sail board at Wingra Canoe and Sailing Center, located in Wingra Park, off Monroe Street, behind Michael's Frozen Custard and the Laurel Tavern.

If you have an urge to canoe on the bigger lakes, you can rent a canoe for about $20 a day from Rutabaga, which is located near the intersection of Monona Drive and the Beltline. A 20-minute paddle up the Yahara River will take you into Squaw Bay and Lake Monona. Heading downstream from Rutabaga will take you under the Beltline Highway bridge and into the cattail marsh of Upper Mud Lake. If you stick to the left-hand shore, you can paddle to the Green Lantern in McFarland for lunch, before heading back. A word to the wise: this is a nice canoe trip during spring and fall. On hot weekend days, there are so many powerboats using the Madison lakes that the water seems more solid than liquid.

It might be the state capitol, but to kids in the summer, Madison's four lakes make the city one big beach.

For Some Beauty and Culture

Another nice spot on Lake Monona is Olbrich Botanical Gardens, located across Atwood Avenue from Olbrich Park (which has a beach, sports fields, and playground equipment). The gardens are free and parents can enjoy the herb, perennial, and rock gardens, while kids run the paths looking for the topiary bush shaped like a bear. Inside, for $1 admission, there is the Bolz Conservancy, which is a tropical rain forest with waterfalls and flying birds.

If you visit Madison when the weather's not so great, check out the campus museums, such as the Geology Museum (great dinosaur fossils, free rocks, and a cave) and Space Place, which has a number of hands-on space activities for children. The Madison Civic Center also has free children's performances on Saturday mornings, called the "Kids in the Crossroads" series.

The Luma Theatre, located on the far East Side, is also a must-see if it has a performance while you're in town. The theater actors perform in the dark, using glowing light to make their eerie art. It's difficult to describe, but a wonderful experience for everyone in the family.

FOR MORE INFORMATION

University of Wisconsin Marching Band Web site, for songs and schedules:
www.wisc.edu/band.

THINGS TO SEE AND DO

Dane County Farmers Market, www.madfarmmkt.org.
Game Haven, 129 State St., (608) 258-8848.
Kohl Center box office (UW athletic tickets), (608) 262-1440.
Luma Theatre, 4535 Helgesen Drive, (608) 222-0077,
www.lumatheatre.com.
Madison Children's Museum, 100 State St., (608) 256-6445.
Olbrich Botanical Gardens, 3330 Atwood Ave., (608) 246-4718.
The Puzzlebox, 230 State St., (608) 251-0701.
Rutabaga, 220 W. Broadway, (608) 223-9300, www.paddlers.com.
State Capitol Tours, (608) 266-0382.
University of Wisconsin Memorial Union, 700 Langdon St., (608) 265-3000.
University of Wisconsin Geology Museum, 1215 W. Dayton St.,
(608) 262-2399.
University of Wisconsin Space Place, 1605 S. Park St., (608) 262-4779.
Wingra Canoe and Sailing Center, Wingra Park, (608) 233-5332.
Wisconsin Veterans Museum, 30 W. Mifflin St., (608) 264-6086.
Wisconsin State Historical Museum, 30 N. Carroll St., (608) 264-6555.

PLACES FOR FOOD

Michael's Frozen Custard, 2531 Monroe St., (608) 231-3500.
Monona Bait & Ice Cream Shop, 4516 Winnequah Rd., (608) 222-1929.

Milwaukee in the Summer

There are zillions of things to do with the whole family in Wisconsin's biggest city on a summer weekend. The problem is deciding what's cool—and what's cool for everyone, especially the kids.

They don't call this the City of Festivals for nothing. We're talking about a season that runs from Asian Moon Festival in early June through Indian Summer in September. Most of the big ones are held at Maier Festival Park (known locally as the Summerfest grounds) along the lakeshore. The carnival and many of the permanent vendors at the park are the same from festival to festival. The other large events are at State Fair Park in West Allis, and at Veteran's Park, which hosts a circus for the week of the Great Circus Parade in July.

Summerfest

Obviously, you can't plan a single weekend around more than one festival, so you should just pick the ones that appeal most to your family.

Take Milwaukee's "Big Gig" itself, otherwise known as Summerfest. The two-week-long festival of food, fun, sun, and music has many things to recommend it for children. Once you pay to get in the gates, you'll find free entertainment ranging from jugglers to magic shows to skateboarding demonstrations. On the negative side, it's usually held during the hottest days of summer, and if you go in the evening when it's cooler, you're going to run into more than a few people who have over-consumed the beverage that made Milwaukee famous. You could treat the whole adventure as a social studies lesson.

First, some advice about getting there. You'll walk a long way—and possibly be stuck in the lot for a long time—if you park at the Summerfest grounds. Instead, you can pick up a shuttle bus from most surrounding counties and from locations inside Milwaukee, ride in air-conditioned comfort, and be dropped right at the front gate. Coming from the west, for example, you can pick up the Wisconsin Coach Lines shuttle at the park-and-ride lot at Highway 83 and Interstate 94 in Delafield. Fare is $4 round trip, and kids like the adventure of taking the bus.

With music, food, and family fun from around the world, Milwaukee's Summerfest offers something for everyone. The festival takes place along the city's beautiful lakefront at the Henry Maier Festival Park. (Photo courtesy of the Greater Milwaukee Convention and Visitor's Bureau.)

Many of the kid-favorite features of Summerfest—ranging from the huge jungle gym park to the amusement park—are permanent attractions at the Maier Festival Park Grounds. So whether you're there in August to enter your daughter in the "red-headed girl" contest at Irish Fest, in mid-July for the Festa Italiana fireworks, or in late July to learn to play sheepshead at German Fest, those attractions will be there.

The amusement park has probably the coolest—in both senses of the word—setting at the park. The rides are on a peninsula sticking out into Lake Michigan, and the giant Ferris wheel provides awesome views of the lake and sunset over the downtown Milwaukee skyline. Be warned, however, that the rides aren't cheap. At $3.75 each, $30 worth of ride tickets will last your average two children under an hour. The best rated ride on a hot day? Either the breeze-producing roller coaster or the splash-creating bumper boats.

Get a Summerfest schedule when you enter, so you won't miss shows such as Truly Remarkable Loon's juggling and comedy act, or the Aggressive Skating Association and their trick skaters. If your kids want to see music, check out the venue ahead of time and get there as much as an hour before show time to stake out good seats. Open air venues such as the Harley Roadhouse are generally better for seeing bands; in smaller venues, the adults leap onto the picnic tables as soon as the music begins, blocking any hope of children actually seeing the performers.

Little shoppers will delight in areas such as the Art Mart, where they can spend hours deciding whether their allowance is best spent on making scented candles or personalized charm bracelets. One year, our best souvenir was an elaborate thread and bead wrap hairdo done by a lady from West Africa. The wrap job cost just $10 and lasted a month, through daily swim team practices.

Four Other Cool Places

The Lakefront Festival of the Arts, located just north of Maier Festival Park on the other side of the Milwaukee Art Museum, is also a great place to take kids. Children are admitted free and they always have fun art activities. One year, kids could paint T-shirts and hats to create wearable art and there was a stage show to keep them entertained while moms and dads browsed the huge show.

If it's a really hot day, head north to Bradford Beach on Milwaukee's lakeshore, where the waters of Lake Michigan are a very quick way to cool off. It's even refreshing to walk out on the breakwater and look at the boats.

Another generally cool spot is the Mitchell Park, home of the famous "Domes." You can rent a rowboat and paddle around the lagoon to enjoy the shade. Because Mitchell Park is part of the National Avenue Mexican-American neighborhood, there are often vendors selling "paleteria," a frozen treat that comes in tropical flavors of mango, pineapple, and coconut.

You can also chill out at the Milwaukee County Zoo, located on Bluemound Road near the intersection with Highway 100. Many of the exhibits are indoors. We like the bird house, where birds fly free, and the reptile house, which is dark and a bit spooky, with all those creatures that slither and have fangs and scales. If it is hot, though, beware, because the zoo is huge and entails a lot of walking. Rent or bring strollers and plan on taking a few rides around the zoo on the mini train, just to rest.

Brewers Baseball

Another fun Milwaukee family experience available most weekends is Milwaukee Brewers baseball. We recommend getting tickets in one of the "family sections," which are scattered throughout the stadium. Family section seats are generally better than average, and they don't allow drinking or smoking. You can't truly appreciate this convenience until you've had to towel off an 8-year-old who got drenched with beer while going for a foul ball.

Ballpark food is expensive, but our favorite treat is "Dippin Dots," tiny very cold balls of ice cream that are mixed to create combinations such as "Banana Split," which contains chocolate, banana, and strawberry balls.

They're served in a souvenir Milwaukee Brewers batting helmet that makes a dandy doll hat once washed.

Look for giveaway and special promotion games—kids can often come home with mini bats, photos with their favorite team player, and even Beanie Babies. There are also deals for the truly cheap. In the County Stadium days, the Brewers offered special family deals on certain games which offered four tickets, four hot dogs, and four sodas for $25. And remember, bleacher seats are still only $5. Considering the cost of NBA tickets, baseball is (pun intended) a steal.

Some years, the Brewers offer deals in conjunction with the Wisconsin State Fair. Bringing your ticket from one will get you a reduced admission at the other. But after a day at the state fair, it is hard to imagine having the energy for a ballgame.

The State Fair—Lots of Good Stuff

Even those who adore the State Fair like to have a strategy for maintaining strength through its miles of exhibits, rides, food, and entertainment. First, you need to plan how to eat your way around the Wisconsin State Fair.

Start early. Lay down a base of something mild, like Cracovia potato pancakes or pirogues. This builds a solid platform to support the spicy and greasy fair food—the Saz ribs, the gyros, the New Berlin Lionesses' Sweet Corn, the funnel cakes, and the cream puffs. Then, of course, there's the stuffed potatoes, "the other burger" (made from pork), and every kind of fried food imaginable.

The fair starts at dawn. At 6 A.M., they start dishing up the Lazybones Farmer Breakfast (the ham is lazy, not the farmers) at the Leinie's Lodge. If that doesn't sound good, there's another stand serving Swedish pancakes with lingonberries, and another pancake breakfast in the exhibit hall.

(Fortunately for the squeamish and the animal rights' lovers, Rupena's no longer serves whole barbecued pig heads. It used to be one of the weirdest sights of the fair, seeing those pig heads—snout, ears and all—rotating sightlessly on the spits.)

Of course, all this leads up to the real reason you're at the Wisconsin State Fair—to eat cream puffs.

Volunteers from the Wisconsin Bakers Association, churn out more than 300,000 cream puffs a year. While you're waiting in line, you can watch the process through glass windows. See the puffs flow from the seasoned copper kettle (in use since cream puffs came to the fair in 1924) through the 38° F "cream room" and right into your mouth.

No kidding. The lines at the cream puff pavilion move so fast that there's no time for virtuous second thoughts. You can fantasize about eating a cream puff, hand $1.50 to one of those nice baker's association people, and be wiping powdered sugar off your nose quicker than it takes to read this.

Vacation Advice

```
E  E  S  C  C  M  N  N  S  A  P  E  T  O  T
L  W  I  S  A  A  C  E  R  L  O  N  S  I  I
O  N  J  T  L  R  K  T  E  E  E  X  D  P  U
P  T  A  C  H  S  D  O  N  R  T  W  E  Z  S
H  H  N  L  V  H  X  S  O  E  C  N  O  G  M
S  S  X  A  O  M  B  G  U  B  T  S  A  T  I
I  A  G  R  L  A  P  C  N  N  G  B  N  L  W
F  N  J  Y  L  L  S  A  T  J  G  N  Y  U  S
Z  D  B  L  Y  L  E  Y  G  N  Q  H  O  A  S
A  A  S  E  D  O  K  P  I  U  T  J  F  S  C
U  L  M  E  K  W  Q  P  E  Y  C  Z  W  B  P
X  S  F  P  U  S  E  O  R  R  E  M  K  I  O
K  L  A  T  W  E  X  H  E  I  P  Z  Z  K  M
Q  N  M  S  L  Z  Z  C  S  K  O  O  B  E  F
V  J  I  S  P  R  C  N  G  H  U  I  M  S  Y
```

BALLS	BIKES	BOOKS
CARDS	FISHPOLE	HAT
LANTERN	MARSHMALLOWS	REPELLANT
SANDALS	SLEEPINGBAGS	SONGBOOK
SUNSCREEN	SWIMSUIT	TENT
TOWELS		

(Solution on page 142)

But don't despair. A monster State Fair Cream Puff is full of fat, but only 165 calories, so you can eat three before you're up into Big Mac calorie territory. Tell kids that the approved way to eat them is to take them apart and eat one half, while giving the other half to your mother.

Once you're totally stuffed, you can wander past the displays of champion cheeses and into the exhibit halls. These are the all-time best places to cool off and entertain kids. There's something very nineteenth-century, and yet mesmerizing, about watching the snake oil salesmen sell stuff that you had no idea you needed. Just don't stare too long at the slicing and dicing, swishing and washing, or you'll be hypnotized into reaching for your credit cards.

Under one air-conditioned roof, you can buy baseball cards and a personality analysis, have your picture taken in Victorian regalia, and pick up shoots that will sprout Hawaiian plumeria so you can make your own leis. And where else can you find topless sandals?

These look like the soles of sandals that some absent-minded cobbler forgot to finish. But they promise to stick to the bottom of your feet—"No hot feet! No blisters! No tan lines!"—and they only set you back $5.

Selling stuff to fairgoers is a tradition that goes back to the peddlers' wagons which pulled into town during the cattle fairs of long ago. There's also the Wonder Knife wizard, who turns potatoes into roses, and cucumbers into sharks. "You can filet fish so fast they'll swim around the bucket naked!"

Once you've had enough of the hard sell, head to the least commercial place at the fair—the shady wildlife park run by the Wisconsin Department of Natural Resources and located in the far southwestern corner of the fair. There's a little river running through it, displays on animals and fish of Wisconsin, and wooden benches where you can rest. You'll also find a schedule of kids' activities which includes things like printing T-shirts with frozen dead fish.

You really haven't seen the fair until you've been to the animal barns. It's fun to see the Jerseys glowing like caramels in their clean hay, and Holsteins hairsprayed and shoe-polished into black and white high contrast.

Check the schedule, because there are usually some show-ring events that appeal to kids. We've spent more than an hour happily entertained by an obstacle course set up for herding dogs. Another time, we found it fascinating to watch a competition between people who decorate draft horses with ribbons and flowers.

One of our favorite ways to rest and to get across the fair is in the Sky Glider, a ski-lift type ride like the one at Summerfest. You might convince little kids that this is the *only* carnival ride. Older ones know there's a whole midway of rides and carnies at the fair. Giving them both a dollar limit and a time limit is probably the only way to assure your sanity.

On the way out, stop by the root beer barrel stand near the park office. Flavored milk, at just a quarter a glass, is one of the best deals of the fair. Sometimes Senator Herb Kohl himself is handing out the cups. Although

Whether it's cream puffs, corn on the cob, or ice cream dots, the Wisconsin State Fair is a great place to eat.

cherry-flavored milk sounds weird, the root beer flavor tastes like a melted root beer float. Pause for a moment and raise a toast to the Wisconsin State Fair, the "Days of Swine and Roses."

THINGS TO SEE AND DO—FESTIVALS

JUNE
CajunFest, Wisconsin State Fair Park, (414) 476-7303.
PrideFest, Henry Maier Festival Park, (414) 645-3378.
West Allis Western Days, Wisconsin State Fair Park, (262) 821-7816.
Asian Moon, Henry Maier Festival Park, (414) 483-8530.
Lakefront Festival of the Arts, Veterans Park, (414) 224-3850.
Polish Fest, Henry Maier Festival Park, (414) 529-2140.
Summerfest, Henry Maier Festival Park, (414) 273-2680.

JULY
Summerfest, Henry Maier Festival Park, (414) 273-2680.
The Great Circus Parade, Downtown Milwaukee, (608) 356-8341.
Festa Italiana, Henry Maier Festival Park, (414) 223-2194.
German Fest, Henry Maier Festival Park, (414) 464-9444.

AUGUST

Wisconsin State Fair, Wisconsin State Fair Park, (414) 266-7000.
African World Festival, Henry Maier Festival Park, (414) 372-4567.
Irish Fest, Henry Maier Festival Park, (414) 476-3378.
Mexican Fiesta, Henry Maier Festival Park, (414) 383-7066.

SEPTEMBER

Indian Summer Festival, Henry Maier Festival Park, (414) 774-7119.
Arabian Fest, Henry Maier Festival Park, (414) 384-4441.

OTHER THINGS TO SEE AND DO

Milwaukee County Zoo, 10001 W. Bluemound Rd., (414) 771-3040.
Milwaukee Brewers, (800) 933-7890, www.milwaukeebrewers.com.
Mitchell Park Horticultural Conservatory, 524 S. Layton Blvd.,
    (414) 649-9830.

See "Milwaukee in the Winter" for a list of even more things to do and a few lodging and eating establishments.

Milwaukee in the Winter

If you can't go to the tropics for the winter, you can go to Milwaukee. After an hour or so of visiting the tropical rain forest and seeing "Amazon" in the virtual reality of the IMAX theater, you'll be wondering if you need malaria medicine. With so much for the whole family to do in Milwaukee, the hard part is figuring out what things you can fit into your weekend agenda.

When in Doubt, Eat

All good campaigns begin on a full stomach, so before you start to tour, you may want to do what my family did—and what President Clinton and German Chancellor Helmut Kohl did before their summit in Milwaukee a few years ago. If you get off I-94 at 13th Street and head back up the Clybourn Street hill, along the edge of the Marquette University campus, you'll find Miss Katie's diner at the top of the hill.

The steel-gray diner looks like it's been there forever, but it hasn't. The Picciurro family, which owns Pitch's restaurants around the Milwaukee metro area, opened it in 1984. The real Miss Katie is the family matriarch.

You can drink a salute to Miss Katie—and watch televised sports—at the long bar while you wait for your table. The kids won't mind waiting, because there's a vintage shuffleboard table and other games to keep them entertained. If there were an award for best view from a one-story downtown building, Miss Katie's would win. Thanks to its hilltop location, it offers a view south across the Menomonee River Valley and east to the Hoan Memorial Bridge and the sparkle of Lake Michigan beyond.

Miss Katie's has a scrapbook of the presidential visit and a rather eerie picture on the wall showing the armed secret service men swarming the rooftop during the presidential visit. If you missed Clinton and Kohl, you'll still see plenty of local and state politicians, reporters, and university types on a regular day at Miss Katie's. And, many will have kids in tow. The scrapbook shows little Ben Norquist, the mayor's boy, pushing back from a big bowl of food on the day of Clinton's visit.

Miss Katie's does treat children well. The staff will make not-on-the-menu favorites, such as grilled cheese sandwiches, and will split one of their huge strawberry malts between two glasses. They even topped each half with whipped cream. You can honor the former president by ordering from the same side of the menu he did: the "presidential appetizer" plate of ribs, buffalo wings, and deep-fried cheese.

Thus fortified, it's time to think about beer.

Suds the Whole Family Can Enjoy

Although Miller has the best-known brewery tour in Milwaukee, it doesn't have the kid-appeal of the second-biggest brewery in beer city, Sprecher. That's because, in addition to beer, Sprecher brews such kid favorites as root beer and cream soda in its brewery, located just off I-43, about five minutes north of downtown. Sprecher was born in 1985 when former Pabst brewing supervisor, and homebrewing enthusiast Randy Sprecher opened up his own microbrewery.

But that's history, and what's interesting is that kids are an important part of Sprecher's future. Sprecher brews more barrels of root beer, cola, and cream soda than beer. On the tour, you'll learn why Sprecher's sodas taste so rich. Sprecher cooks the honey, sugar, botanicals, and other flavorings in the same copper kettles used for cooking the beer wort. The honey and sugar caramelize at the bottom, creating a deeper flavor than the cold-mix used at mainstream soda companies.

Although the kids like the end of the tour—the part when they could have all the soda they could drink—the half-hour tour, with its technical explanations of beer making steps, may seem long. You will need reservations for the tours, which are given on Friday and Saturday afternoons.

Winding Down at Mitchell Park

If all that soda gives children a sugar buzz, you might want to work it off at Mitchell Park Conservatory, known as "the domes" to everyone young and old.

Although you may not think your kids have a deep appreciation of horticulture, think about this: if your little body spent half the year encased in heavy snowpants, jackets, boots, hats, mittens, and scarves, wouldn't you love the chance to shuck it all and run free in the warmth among tropical trees?

Many kids love the domes, which include a rainforest, a desert, and a seasonal dome with displays, such as massive model railroad setups, that usually appeal to children.

Or, if you've had enough touring, retire to your hotel and make sure it has a pool. The west suburbs near the Brookfield Square shopping center seem to have a plethora of "swimming pool hotels" geared toward families. And the good news is that you're near that all-time great kids eatery, Fuddrucker's, located near the busy corner of Moorland and Bluemound roads. Fuddrucker's features top-quality burgers designed by you, and grilled before your eyes, before you garnish them with as much (or, in the case of children, as little) as you like. There's a separate make-your-own taco area, where the grill chef will throw on a marinated skirt steak and make you one of the best "carne asada" burritos north of National Avenue. In the morning, kids may have time for another swim before heading down to the museums.

Betty Brinn Children's Museum

Families with younger children should check out the Betty Brinn Children's Museum, located near the lakefront at 929 E. Wisconsin Avenue. Toddlers can splash in sand and water and explore a large barge while checking out the real boats on Lake Michigan.

The children's museum also has exhibits on the workings of the human body. Kids can listen to digestion and crawl through a giant human heart. Most kids seem to happily do the sliding and crawling without learning a thing, but the exhibit that lets them weave a scab on the great wall of skin might be memorable if only because the concept is disgusting enough to get their attention.

Milwaukee Public Museum

Those with older children should head directly to the Milwaukee Museum complex, located at West Wells Street and Seventh Avenue in downtown Milwaukee. Baby boomer parents can reminisce about when the museum opened

The central focus of the Milwaukee Public Museum's Butterfly Garden includes a 2,000-square-foot vivarium featuring several species of live butterflies, flowering plants, and a waterfall. (Photo courtesy of the Milwaukee Convention and Visitors Bureau and the Milwaukee Public Museum.)

in the 1960s. A lot of it looks familiar, although we found it distressing that the naked boy in the fountain who used to make us giggle is gone. The Streets of Old Milwaukee are still there—the same old lady is rocking on her porch!—and so is the secret button, hidden in the rocks of the buffalo stampede diorama, that makes the rattlesnake shake his tail.

Today's kids have their own traditions to revisit. In the museum's rain forest display, which opened in the late 1980s, they race to be the first to push the button that makes a howler monkey come screaming out of the tropical treetops. Distressingly, one child referred to the look on the monkey's face as "mommy in the morning."

Kids could literally spend all day inside the rain forest, lingering over displays of iridescent butterflies, watching videos, answering questions in the flip displays, and trying to figure out if the giant Aripima fish could swallow dad whole.

Be warned that the entrance to the rain forest can be scary for little kids. There's a giant tyrannosaurus ripping the guts out of a triceratops, as lightning flashes and dinosaur snorts and groans are broadcast through the room. Kids that would rather miss the "scary dinosaur breeving" can come in the back of the exhibit, off the museum's main hall.

Discovery World and Humphrey IMAX Theater

The museum is now connected to Discovery World Museum and Humphrey IMAX Dome Theater, which makes it tough to visit the whole complex in one afternoon. It's less expensive to do all three as part of a combo ticket and it's a good idea to purchase your IMAX theater tickets at the same time as your museum admission because the hourly shows tend to sell out.

You can spend the time before your IMAX show on Discovery World's second floor, where a display on "Milwaukee Muscle" demonstrates both the city's famous blue collar heritage and the basic laws of physics. Kids can learn how to heft a 100-pound fieldstone by making the lever longer and have fun hoisting themselves up and down in the type of a pulley chair used for ascending ship masts.

Others will like the electricity demonstrations like the water wheel and power house. Kids control water flowing into a large, enclosed waterwheel, then use the electricity they generate to light a series of translucent homes. It even includes a bit of Wisconsin history: did you know that our country's first water-powered generating plant was built in Appleton in 1882?

In Area 51, kids can pretend to test pilot the shuttle mission. Kids have to work together, giving commands to the one wearing the helmet camera. This can be fun, but not an activity for arguing siblings.

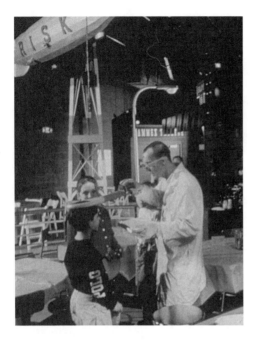

In the Discovery World Museum, kids and adults can explore clouds, build a robot, or watch a lightning bolt. Over 140 hands-on exhibits and live theater shows keep everyone enthralled for hours. (Photo courtesy of the Greater Milwaukee Convention and Visitors Bureau and Discovery World.)

When it's time for your movie, get your hands stamped for readmission before crossing the hall to the six-story tall IMAX movie theater. Frankly, I was a little worried. The shows start with a bang: a preview showing a wild helicopter ride over and around the buildings of downtown Milwaukee. Because the giant screen wraps around viewers and the sound system is powerful enough to move air, you really felt like you were flying. Adults have been seen cringing and ducking to avoid ramming into the Firstar Tower.

Feature films change regularly. A recent one on the Amazon River conjured enough deep jungle mist and trilling bird sounds to make you feel you were there. The Everest film is returning, and the theater also has scheduled films on dolphins, Egypt, and Hemingway's "Old Man in the Sea." The Milwaukee IMAX has decided not to show the new version of Disney's "Fantasia," sticking with its repertoire of science and educational movies.

After the movie, you can check Discovery World to see if it's offering special events, such as "family fusion workshops." These family learning events are designed for the family to work as a team to learn and have fun. Sometimes you'll follow a treasure map through the museum looking for clues, while other times you may have to solve puzzles based on the exhibits.

Discovery World also has its own theater, with shows such as "Electro," which teaches about electricity.

Many kids like settling in at the stainless steel counters of the R&D Cafe. At this cleverly designed station, kids can "order" science experiments from a menu for a minimal fee, ranging from 75 cents for a soldering kit to 25 cents for "invention dissection," an old appliance and enough screwdrivers to take it apart.

The cafe offers such experiments as making "homemade" GAK—a slimy, jelly-like substance children pay big money for in toy stores. At the R&D cafe, a quarter buys a recipe, a tray full of ingredients, and measuring tools.

You can also make foil art pictures, using a heat wand to fuse copier toner and foil film. Nearby, kids don safety goggles and use machines and metal-working tools to turn a sheet of copper into necklace medallions. Most kids leave Discovery World clutching an armload of handmade souvenirs: necklaces, treasure maps, foil art, and plastic bags filled with GAK. The fact that they already have their goodies cuts down on the traditional whining at the gift shop.

Don't leave town without indulging in another classic Milwaukee treat: frozen custard. It seems that there are almost as many custard stands in Milwaukee as neighborhood taverns, and each has its followers. In the winter, head south to 27th Street and Oklahoma, where Leon's has been dishing up this decadent treat since 1942. Although Leon's is only a drive-in, it's open every day of the year except Christmas.

THINGS TO SEE AND DO

Betty Brinn Children's Museum, 929 E. Wisconsin Ave., (414) 291-0888.
(Children and adults, $2.)
Bradley Center, 1001 N. Fourth St., (414) 227-0400.
Discovery World Museum, 712 W. Wells St., (414) 765-0777.
(Adults $5.50, seniors 60 and over $4.50, children 4 and older $4.),
www.discoveryworld.com.
Humphrey IMAX Dome Theater, 800 W. Wells St., (414) 319-IMAX.
(Adults $6.50, seniors $5.50, children 3 and over $5.),
www.humphreyimax.com.
Miller Brewing Co., 4251 W. State St., free tours, (414) 931-BEER.
Milwaukee Public Museum, 800 W. Wells St., (414) 278-2700.
(Adults $6.50, seniors $5, children 4 and over $4.), www.mpm.edu.
Mitchell Park Conservatory, 524 S. Layton Blvd., (414) 649-9800. (Adults
$4, seniors and children over 6, $2.50.)
Sprecher Brewing Co., 701 W. Glendale Ave., (414) 964-2739.
(Adults $2, children 20 and under $1.)

PLACES TO STAY

Embassy Suites, 1200 S. Moorland Rd., Brookfield, (262) 782-2900.
Midway Hotel, 251 N. Mayfair Rd., Milwaukee, (800) 528-1234.
Milwaukee Hilton, 509 W. Wisconsin Ave., (414) 271-7250.
Days Inn, 11811 W. Bluemound Rd., (800) 329-7466.

PLACES FOR FOOD

Miss Katie's Diner, 1900 W. Clybourn St., (414) 344-0044.
Leon's Frozen Custard, 3131 S. 27th St., (414) 383-1784.
Fuddrucker's, 16065 W. Bluemound Rd., Brookfield, (262) 784-3833

Waushara and Marquette Counties

Despite billboards that hype the thrills of Wisconsin resorts to travelers before they cross the Illinois border, some of the best weekends for families are found in places less known.

It may seem as though there's not much going on in the sand country of northern Marquette and southern Waushara counties—and that's just the point. This is an old-fashioned, make your own fun in the summer kind of place, as those who vacation on the area's small sandy lakes and beautiful trout streams know well.

Biking the Rural Roads

For one thing, the area, roughly equidistant from Milwaukee, Madison, and Green Bay, offers some of the best family biking in Wisconsin. You'll probably want to get a backroads map and plan your own itinerary. Roads are paved and rolling, but not hilly. If you bike the roads between, say, Dakota and Richford, you'll pass fields of prairie grasses and roadside displays of wildflowers, such as spicy blue bee balm and bright orange lilies. There are cool, piney spots where the roads cross the Mecan River, perfect to stop and dip your feet into the cool water. In fall and spring, it's not uncommon to pass fields where the grazing sandhill cranes outnumber the cattle.

There's so little traffic that the only vehicles passing you may be Amish buggies. The area has been settled by the Amish, so many of the farms will have horses, plain white farmhouses, and kids playing outside wearing bonnets and straw hats. If you're lucky, you'll be able to pedal past as Amish farmers are plowing with workhorses or gathering wheat into shocks to dry in the field. It may get children thinking about how everyone lived 100 years ago—and how their own lives would be different without electricity, cars, and other conveniences we take for granted.

If you're really lucky, you'll see a sign announcing an Amish bakery at one of the farms. Look for homemade noodles, pies, and some of the best raised donuts this side of heaven. (One bakery has operated about 2 miles north of Richford on Highway B, but these things change, so ask around.)

On Highway JJ just west of Highway B, there's a game farm where bikers can pause and watch a herd of huge elk graze behind a fence.

Kids, being observant, might notice the road signs of central Wisconsin. Road names like Cottonville, Cumberland, Cypress, and Dixie sound like they belong in the south, but they're part of a system that alphabetizes roads from north to south through several counties.

Get Out on the Water

If you pedal towards Richford, you might want to bring your swimsuit for a stop at Curtis Lake, a small county park beach on one of the area's many sandy, shallow, and clean lakes. On a hot Sunday, you may hear an Amish buggy clatter down the road and pull up to the beach, so the children can cool off by wading.

Besides Curtis Lake, Marl Lake between Hancock and Wautoma, and the local park in Mount Morris are also great swimming holes for kids, and they offer shady hillsides for picnics. But for "make your own fun" equal to the thrills and chills of a much more expensive waterpark, go to the quarries of the Redgranite area. At the turn of the century, Redgranite was famous for its red rock, which was mined for paving stones. When the rock went out of style in the 1920s, the owners quit pumping the ground water out of the quarries and they filled with water.

Quarry Park in Redgranite, behind the post office, is a great place for a dip on a hot day and a favorite with scuba divers who explore its clear water to look at the mining equipment in the depths. The park is a place where you'll find bright red cliffs and clear blue water, cliff diving and rope swings. What you won't find is any shallow water, making the quarry a better spot for teens and children who are excellent deepwater swimmers. Small children should wear life vests. One favorite sunny day activity is floating on an inner tube, face near the water, and paddling slowly along the cliff's walls, looking down, down, down, to see the fish swimming in the depths.

The area abounds with other watery weekend activities. You might bring inner tubes and float one of the area's larger trout streams. Putting in on the Mecan River at the Highway 22 bridge west of Dakota and floating down to the next bridge, on 14th Avenue near the Lake of the Woods campground, takes about three hours and is perfect for kids over age five or so, because the water is seldom more than three feet deep. The White River above the White River Campground at Highway YY is also nice for tubing.

While you're floating, you can tell kids the famous story of the runaway hippo of the Mecan. Way back in the spring of 1994, some trout fisherman came around a bend in the river and discovered, much to their surprise, a

The Mecan River isn't just great for trout fishing, it's also a wonderful way to spend a hot afternoon in an inner tube.

dead hippopotamus in the middle of the creek. They called police, who eventually discovered that the hippo had started out at the R-Zoo game farm near Neshkoro. The owner told police that the camel and the hippo were in a pen together, and that the camel must have worked the lock and released the hippo to go on a walkabout around the county.

The hippo apparently wandered about for several days, before it hunkered down in the Mecan about five miles from where it started. When the owner found it, and couldn't get it out of the water, he shot it and called the stock truck. After the story came out, people admitted that they had seen the hippo lumbering around, but didn't want to say anything for fear their friends would think they were nuts.

There's apparently a tavern near Germania that serves a "hippo burger" in honor of the fallen beast.

For those who want to tangle with the wily trout, the Waushara and Marquette County area is a paradise of public fishing areas on streams such as the Wedde, the Chaffee, the White River, and Willow Creek. Maps showing public fishing areas on these streams and others are available from the state Department of Natural Resources and most bait and fishing license outlets.

Fun Places for Food and Lodging

All this activity will get the family water-logged and hungry, so you might want to head to Wautoma, where your children can order shakes and fries at the Milty Wilty on Highway 21 on the eastern edge of town—an old-fashioned drive-in with a great name. Or, if it's Saturday, head south to the little town of Spring Lake and see if Mattie's Bakery, run by an Amish woman, is still operating in the old general store. If it is, don't leave without a few sacks of cookies—the big soft peanut butter cookies and the oatmeal-chocolate chip concoctions are highly recommended.

For places to stay in the area, you'll have to go for cottages, motels, or private campgrounds, because there aren't any state parks in the area. The family-run "Lake of the Woods" campground, just east of Dakota near the Mecan River, offers a swimming pool, a fishing pond, mini-golf, and splash boat and canoe trips on the Mecan River.

If you prefer camping on one of the area's sandy lakes, check out the To-morrow Wood Campground on Fish Lake near Hancock, the Evergreen Campsite on Kusel Lake (also the site of a family restaurant and a nice county beach) near Wild Rose, or Flanagan's Pearl Lake Campsites, near Redgranite.

Try breakfast at the Royal Cafe in Coloma, a tiny red box of a restaurant, located on Highway 21 just east of I-39. One bite of their pancakes will show you why they've been in business more than 50 years.

Fairs and Festivals

For evening entertainment, get a copy of the Central Wisconsin Resorter, and see which small town has a festival. (The "Coloma Chicken-Chew" has the best title.) If you're visiting during the second weekend in July, don't miss the Marquette County Fair which is held in Westfield. It's the quintessential small town fair—animals rest in a historic round barn, the 4-H kids sell malts for $1, and the local farm ladies serve up an excellent $5 fried chicken supper. Parking and admission are free, the rides are much cheaper than those at more urban fairs, and it has a great small-town feeling.

The much larger Waushara County fair, held the third weekend of August in Wautoma, is

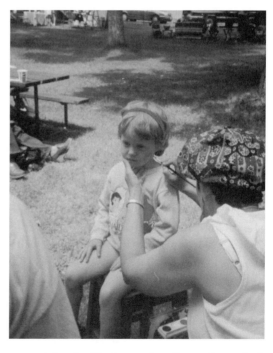

Every July, the Black Hawk Folk Music Festival brings live music and face painting to the park in tiny Mount Morris.

also a good one. The Black Hawk Folk Music Festival, held the second weekend in July at Mount Morris Park, brings in well-known performers. Children get in free, and as an added bonus, you can float around the lake in inner tubes while listening to the music.

Some Great Land-Locked Activities

For more serious studies of nature, the Mecan Discovery Center, located on the river about halfway between Wautoma and Montello on Dixie Lane off Highway 22, could be a great family base for area adventures. It has rustic cabins, canoe and tube trips, and offers classes on wildlife and other nature topics. During the summer, it offers a series of free "Wild Wednesday" programs. Ask about the suggested 9-mile bike loop starting and ending at the Discovery Center, a shady jaunt that takes you along several area trout streams.

Waushara County is also a nice home base for experimental airplane buffs planning to attend the annual EAA Air-Adventure held each year at Oshkosh's Wittmann Field. Wautoma is just 30 minutes from Oshkosh via Highway 21. And if you miss the annual fly-in—usually held the last week of July and first week of August—the EAA Air Adventure Museum is open year round.

Kids who want to learn about the early pioneers of flight can see exhibits on the Wright Brothers, Charles Lindbergh, and World War II fighter pilots. In the summer, Pioneer Airport, a recreation of an early flying field, is open, and brave people can book flights on an open cockpit biplane or a vintage airliner.

Check Out Montello

For those who would rather snare a shopping bargain than a fish, Montello is worth exploring. Children like the man-made waterfalls in Granite Park downtown, and there are several antique stores worthy of prowling.

The B&B Country Store in Montello is children's paradise. There's an ice cream counter and dozens of bins holding a boggling array of candy. Kids can get paper bags and fill them with: saltwater taffy, Montello mints, caramel bull's eyes, root beer barrels, Necco wafers, peanut butter kisses, sour balls, and candy buttons on paper. It's not penny candy anymore—most pieces cost a nickel—but children can get a lot of candy for a dollar. And if you're fretting about their teeth, just console yourself with the thought that getting the maximum amount of candy for a buck is great for kids' math skills. Look up on the wall and you'll see an antique "chuck wagon" kitchen that was designed to ride on the back of a covered wagon.

Around the corner, you'll find Buffalo Books, where you can order coffee drinks and sip them on a flower-bedded deck overlooking the Montello River. There's an excellent collection of local books featuring hometown celebrities such as John Muir, and a collection of maps of the area that are a nice find for canoeists, bikers, and hikers. Select from their nice selection of children's books, and the kids can read in the car on the way home, the perfect end to a make-your-own-fun weekend.

FOR MORE INFORMATION

Montello Area Chamber of Commerce, 640 Main St., Montello, WI 53949 (800) 684-7199, or www.palacenet.net/montello/chamber.

Wautoma Area Chamber of Commerce, P.O. Box 65, Wautoma, WI 54982 (877) WAUTOMA, www.wautoma.com/chamber.

Westfield Chamber of Commerce, P.O. Box 393, Westfield, WI 53964 (608) 296-4146, www.maqs.net/~westflcc/direct.html.

THINGS TO SEE AND DO

B & B Country Store, 28 W. Montello St., Montello, (608) 297-7511.

EAA Air Adventure Museum, 3000 Poberezny Rd., Oshkosh, (920) 426-4800, www.eaa.org.

Mecan River Discovery Center, W3281 Dixie Ave., Neshkoro, WI 54960, (920) 293-8404.

PLACES TO STAY

Lake of the Woods Campground, N9070 14th Ave., Wautoma, WI 54982, (920) 787-3601 or (888) 919-9109. E-mail: lotw3601@aol.com.

section 3
The Southwest

The Dells in the Summer

Mention Wisconsin Dells to a kid and you'll probably get whoops of delight. Mention it to a parent, and you may get eye rolling and an involuntary pat of the wallet, just to make sure it's still there.

Yes, you can go to the Dells for a weekend, get stuck in traffic, and spend a lot of money while sweating, but the Dells/Baraboo area also has plenty of low-cost, back-to-nature activities that will please children and parents alike.

Touring the Dells by Water

The first and best advice to Dells-goers is this: get down to the water any way you can. You can be distracted by the millions of lurid billboards and miss the whole reason the Dells became a vacation attraction in the first place—the beautiful rock gorges cut by the Wisconsin River. You really need to see them up close to appreciate the centuries-old lure of the place.

Probably the easiest way to take in the river scenery is on a Duck or boat ride. The Ducks are World War II vintage vehicles that go from land to water and back, on a tour of the Lower Dells. The ride is bumpy and pseudo-adventurous, so kids like it, and the geology of the area—which includes rock formations such as the Sugar Bowl—is explained in a way that children can understand.

You can take boat tours of the Upper Dells—with stops at Witch's Gulch and Stand Rock, and views of High Rock and Romance Cliff. Both boat and duck tours take about an hour, and give kids a good overview of the river and the legends of its past.

A more adventurous way to see the water is to canoe the Dells yourself. A one-hour paddle starts at the boat landing below the dam on the east side of the river (you'll have to carry your canoe down a steep hill). Once you're afloat, look for the giant iron ring bolted high into the rock. This is where raftsmen would tie their lumber rafts, so they could reassemble the wood after the hairy trip over the Kilbourn dam.

Further down river on the western shore, you'll see pilings that mark the ruins of a German beer garden. This is all that's left of the lost village of Newport, which moved upriver over the ice after losing the derby for the railroad bridge in the 1850s. You can end your trip at the Highway A boat landing, where Lake Delton empties into the river.

Some Great Hiking

You can also hike to some of the Upper Dells' prettiest natural spots through 1,070 acres of land acquired by the state in 1994. Once you cross the river into Wisconsin Dells, take the first left on River Road heading north out of town. The state parking lot is just past the Birchcliff Resort. A 2-mile round trip hike into Chapel Gorge will take you to a rocky promontory on the Narrows, a good spot for a picnic and sight seeing.

Once you arrive, you'll see the Dells the way Indians and explorers saw it: blue brown waves of river water churning against canyon walls of sandstone. The beach itself is a crescent of flood-cleansed reddish sand, decorated only with a large driftwood tree and a couple of beer bottles left behind by boaters. The beach has long been popular with boaters, but wasn't accessible by land until the state built the trail.

A state property, Crandall Pines on River Road, north of Chapel Gorge, is a hike through 140,000 pines planted in the 1920s by George Crandall, who bought much of the land that now makes up the Dells of the Wisconsin State Natural Area to protect it from further destruction. (The Kilbourn Dam at Wisconsin Dells, built in 1908 at the urging of developers with grandiose schemes for the area, had already drowned the islands and features like Giant's Hand and Diamond Grotto in the upper Dells.)

Crandall worked to reforest the land, and his children gave the land and the Dells Boat Company to the Wisconsin Alumni Research Foundation in 1954. Forty years later, WARF sold the land to the DNR at a below market value to guarantee its protection. The boat company has a lease to continue running boat tours up the side canyons of the river.

Crandall was the son-in-law of famed landscape photographer H.H. Bennett, who saved the Dells he loved another way: by preserving it forever in sumptuous photos of its unique landmarks. Be sure to check out the H.H. Bennett Studio and History Center in downtown Wisconsin Dells, which has been restored to its 1908 appearance, complete with original darkroom and equipment. The History Center features Bennett's images and a re-creation of a riverboat trip through the Dells in the early 1900s.

Those Wonderful Water Parks

No kid's summer trip to the Dells could be considered complete without a visit to one of the mega water parks. In addition to the growing list of water parks that are part of hotels, there are three major destination water parks—Riverview Park, Family Land, and Noah's Ark.

Each park has its devotees and specialties. Riverview is generally the least expensive and the best bet for the youngest children, or on colder days. Admission to Riverview includes go-karts and other carnival style activities for kids who don't love the water.

Family Land is a favorite of—guess what—families, especially those with an age range. There are three large water play areas for younger kids and nearby tables where families can picnic and watch the little ones. Older kids will like the speed slides, mini-golf, and giant wave pool.

For teenagers, and older kids, there's no place like Noah's Ark. America's biggest water park adds new attractions every year and advertises heavily, so kids know about the Flash Flood, Dark Voyage, and the Big Kahuna ahead of time. There are little kid areas, too, but to get your money's worth (and because it always seems to be crowded and congested), you'll want to save Noah's until the kids are older.

They look like giant sea shells and frogs and dolphins, but if you're in the Wisconsin Dells in the summer, they're probably water slides.

Next, a word about water park strategy. Family Land and Riverview both advertise that families can bring their own picnics, while Noah's does not. However, Noah's doesn't seem to care that dozens of families bring in coolers full of food and drink and park them under the picnic tables. Do this and you'll save a lot on what can be an expensive day.

Second, get there early and scope out the crowd. If it's already hot, you don't want to pick a ride that will result in a long wait in line before you get wet. The rule of thumb seems to be: the larger the raft, the longer the line. Thus, attractions such as Kowabunga, Dark Voyage, and Flash Flood can have waits of an hour or more. If you just want to get cool, the Endless River, Adventure River, and the two wave pools will give fast relief.

Some rides, however, are worth the wait. While you're waiting for your turn on the Flash Flood ride, you can get repeatedly drenched by the waves that wash over the bridge.

For any of the water parks, remember to reapply sun block throughout the day, bring hats and T-shirts for fair-skinned kids, and pick a meeting spot in case you get separated.

It's not a water park, but another not-to-be-missed area attraction with a water theme is the Tommy Bartlett Thrill Show, where you sit under the tall white pines on Lake Delton's western shore and watch water skiers do their tricks. Kids really like this show—which seems better than what some Baby Boomer parents will remember from their youths. Bartlett, the old wizard of Wisconsin Dells, is now water-skiing in another realm, but his show goes on.

Southward to Baraboo

Beyond the commercial attractions, the area offers a wealth of fun educational opportunities. The International Crane Foundation, located just east of Highway 12 between the Dells and Baraboo, offers tours and videos about saving these endangered birds. Kids who have visited for school field trips seem to enjoy showing their families around.

Another truly great family value is Circus World Museum in Baraboo. Located on the site of the Ringling Brothers summer grounds, the museum gives families a great chance to see a real circus without the tawdriness of the

Whether it's fake elephants or real ones performing under the big top, Circus World Museum in Baraboo is a great place to see the beasts. And don't miss the daily elephant "splash around" in the Baraboo River.

travel troupes. There are daily Big Top performances during the summer, and although the kids don't always have a huge interest in circus history, they love the "elephant splash-around," a daily event in which the behemoths wade into the Baraboo River for their daily bath. A family can easily spend a whole day at Circus World.

A Night at Devils Lake

If it's Saturday night and you want to escape the crowds, you might want to take the family over to the Chateau at Devils Lake, located south of Baraboo. It offers big band music on Saturday nights from mid-June to Labor Day. The sweetest time to hear the music is at sundown, just before the sun leaves the lake valley and warms the East Bluff cliffs to a buttery glow. You can float out onto the lake in your inner tube, listening to Tommy Dorsey's arrangement of "Sunnyside" come drifting across the water.

Of course, if you never get out of the water and go inside the Chateau, you'll miss what has been called "Wisconsin's most romantic dance hall." The Chateau, located on the north beach of Devils Lake State Park, has been the place to dance in the moonlight since the Earl Morse Band began playing there in 1925. Take a turn around the floor with Daddy's little girl. Even kids who dislike dancing will like browsing through the Chateau's gift shop full of candy and souvenirs.

Another excellent entertainment value is the Big Sky Twin Drive-In Theater, located a few miles south of Wisconsin Dells on Highway 16. It's one of just a handful of drive-in movie theaters left in the state—and a great way to show kids what Mom and Dad did when they were young.

If you're thinking about camping for the night, be aware that Devils Lake State Park is the second most popular park in the state system, so you might find campsites hard to come by, or crowded and noisy when you do get one. Some families prefer the Mirror Lake State Park which, even though its closer to the Dells and I-90/94, often seems more peaceful. Located on the steep, wooded shores of Mirror Lake, the park has a nice beach, three campgrounds, a boat launch, and a fishing pier. Rocky gorges make canoe trips around the lake especially scenic.

Hiking the Baraboo Hills

Another non-commercial way to enjoy the area is to hike through the Baraboo Hills, one of the wildest spots in southern Wisconsin. Parfrey's Glen, a deep gorge in the hills, is especially suitable for children, because a short walk will take you deep into another world. In winter, icicles hang from the steep rock sides, while in summer, the glen is a cool ferny spot, even when the temperature is beastly. The glen is located between Devils Lake and Merrimac. From Devils Lake, take DL to Highway 113, then south to where DL goes east towards Devil's Head Ski Resort. The parking lot for Parfrey's Glen will be on your left.

Nearby is the Old Schoolhouse restaurant, a good kid-friendly place to get deep-dish pizza before heading home. Take the free Merrimac Ferry across the river if you can—it's the last free ferry in the state and constantly, it seems, in danger of being replaced by a bridge. If there's a line on the north shore, don't fret. It means you'll have time to stock up on ice cream cones and popcorn at the stand before crossing.

On the way home, fortify yourself and your family with a bag of "cow pies" from the Baraboo Candy Company, located across Highway 12 from Ho-Chunk Casino. As the sign says, "A day without cow pies is Un-Baraboo."

THINGS TO SEE AND DO

Big Sky Twin Drive-in Theater, Highway 16 East, Wisconsin Dells, (608) 254-8025.

Chateau at Devils Lake State Park, Baraboo, (608) 356-3381.

Circus World Museum, 550 Water St., Baraboo, (608) 356-0800.

Dells Boat Tours, 11 Broadway, Wisconsin Dells, (608) 254-8555.

Family Land, 1701 Wisconsin Dells Parkway, Wisconsin Dells, (608) 254-7766, www.wisdellstreasureisland.com.

International Crane Foundation, E-11376 Shady Lane, Baraboo, (608) 356-9462.

Noah's Ark, 1410 Wisconsin Dells Parkway, Wisconsin Dells, (608) 254-6351, www.noahsarkwaterpark.com.

Original Wisconsin Ducks, 1890 Wisconsin Dells Parkway, Wisconsin Dells, (608) 254-8751.

Riverview Park, Highway 12, Wisconsin Dells, (608) 254-2608, www.riverviewpark.com.

Tommy Bartlett Thrill Show, 560 Wisconsin Dells Parkway, (608) 254-2525, www.tommybartlett.com.

PLACES TO STAY

Devils Lake State Park, S5975 Park Rd., Baraboo, (608) 356-8301.

Mirror Lake State Park, E-10320 Fern Dell Rd., Baraboo, (608) 254-2333.

PLACES FOR FOOD

Baraboo Candy Company, Highway 12, (608) 356-7425.

Old Schoolhouse, corner of Highway DL and Bluff Rd., Merrimac, (608) 493-2339.

The Dells in the Winter

The race is on, and who could have predicted it? It used to be that on Labor Day, they rolled up the sidewalks in the Dells and got ready to hibernate. Not anymore.

Water Parks of the Mega Variety

These days, the family can spend a great winter weekend in the Dells, because of a new kind of tourist trap undreamed of a decade ago—the indoor water park. Yes, the people who invented "duck rides," fudge shops, and water-ski shows to pull money out of your pocket have devised a way to have you wearing a bathing suit and sliding down a waterslide 365 days a year.

Who cares if it's winter outside? It's warm and tropical inside the many indoor water parks in Wisconsin Dells.

And it's working. The indoor water park hotels are racing to be the biggest, the best, the newest, and the most thrilling. This results in the Dells being packed much of the winter. Room rates can be as high—and reservations as difficult to come by—at the end of February as they are at the beginning of August.

Anyone who has spent a Wisconsin winter trapped indoors with children can understand the attraction. With the Northern Hemisphere tilted away from the sun, the real lakes are frozen and the real world has turned slushy gray. Suddenly, a day in warm water with a piña colada for Mom and water slides for the children seems like a great idea. (Even if the rates and two-day mandatory booking policies make you wonder if it would have been cheaper to just fly to Florida.)

The trend began with the Polynesian. In the hyper-competitive world of Wisconsin Dells tourism, others soon followed suit. Existing hotels such as Antigua Bay, Chula Vista, and Copacabana added indoor parks, and others sprang up all over the Wisconsin Dells Parkway.

Inside the Family Land and Treasure Island Water Park resort complex, the 50,000-square-foot Bay of Dreams lets you slide through Mayan ruins and a faux jungle with masks and statues. Mom and Dad get cozy in the Jaguar's Chamber Spa while the little kids play on the "Hispaniola," a pirate ship.

If that's too tropical for your taste, you can head over to the Kalahari, where the theme is the African desert and veldt. The Kalahari promises to be the first of the indoor parks that lets you visit for a daily fee, a plus for families who want to stay elsewhere, but crave a few hours of water park fun.

Other indoor water park resorts include The Wilderness (which held the biggest Dells title, for a few months in 2000), Atlantis, Raintree, and Blizzard Bay at the Wintergreen Resort.

Get a Taste of the North Woods—Indoors

The Great Wolf Lodge (known as the Black Wolf Lodge prior to mid-2000) is a pseudo northern affair located right on I-90/94. It has more than 42,000 square feet of water park and 309 guest rooms, but it's going to have to scramble to keep up with the even newer parks. Jack Waterman, who founded Noah's Ark and the original Black Wolf, says the goal isn't sheer size, but rather the more esoteric aim of "making family memories worth repeating."

Did they succeed? The first impression was a good one. The log and totem pole exterior gives way to a four-story lobby decorated in "Ye Olde Lodge" style. A fire burns in the stone fireplace, and stuffed moose, bear, and owls snarl from their perches, while lights twinkle from a chandelier that appears to be made of elk horns. It might be "fake Up North," but as a friend used to say about her pearl necklace, it's a good fake.

In the Dells

Across
3. Separates Upper Dells from Lower.
4. Rock sided canyons.
6. Ride one from land to water.
7. Name of local Indian nation.
8. Makes the slides faster.
Down
1. Where the dog jumps.
2. A chocolate treat.
5. Tommy Bartlett has one.

(Solution on page 142)

All of this was lost on children who streak through the lobby to the indoor water park beyond.

Shouts of "Cool!" and "Awesome!" are heard routinely from first-time visitors. The water really is quite a sight. Mammoth water slides, some big enough to carry double-rider inner tubes, disgorge squealing kids. Other kids floated around the "lazy river," played basketball, or tried to stay aboard floating fiberglass animals. There's a 12-level tree house with 60 water activities, plus three more slides, and an entire park of outdoor slides, pools, and toys, should you visit when the weather is warmer.

One great unadvertised secret of these resorts is that everyone else present is either a parent or a child. The moms all look like they've given birth to one or two children, and the dads have bellies that lap comfortably over their swim trunks. It's a lot less intimidating wearing a swimsuit here than, say, the hard-body beach at Cancun.

When children tire of the water, they can visit the game room just across from the pools, featuring what looks like an acre of buzzing, whirring, flashing arcade games. The huge plastic cow, that you "milk" to earn tokens, is a big hit with visitors to America's Dairyland. The games seem generous with the tokens, and $5 per kid will keep them occupied for more than an hour. At the end of their play, they can exchange tokens for some fairly decent prizes.

There are enough contraptions, activities, and games in the Great Wolf Lodge's indoor water park to keep kids occupied for hours.

A double queen fireplace suite, at $235 for six people, is a mid-range accommodation at Great Wolf. Rooms are also decorated in "Ye Olde Lodge" style, with miniature snowshoe lamps, a stone fireplace, and bathroom wallpaper in a "Boundary Waters" motif. Nice features for families include a mini-refrigerator, coffee maker, and microwave. Rooms range from $139 for a single king bed during the week to $299 for the deluxe loft fireplace suite on a winter weekend night. The lodge sometimes requires a two-night stay if you booked for a Saturday night.

It's not cheap, but it's also less expensive than, say, flying a family of four to Florida for a mid-winter retreat. It's also not bad by Dells standards because a family of four would spend close to $100 for a single day at the water park during the summer. At Great Wolf and other water park hotels, admission to the pools is included in the room rent.

Although Great Wolf offers a full-service family restaurant, families too tired to consider getting dressed and going out again can call room service for pizza. The two pizzas, cheese for the kids and vegetarian for the parents, cost $27 including tip.

In the morning, there's barely time to swim, because the pools don't open until 9 A.M. and check-out is at 10:30 A.M. The pool opening time may sound early, but the hours between when the first cartoon flicks on at 6 A.M. and the pool opens can seem much longer in a room full of children.

Skiing for the Whole Family

There are, of course, more seasonal activities in the Dells area in the winter. If your family likes cross-country skiing, both Mirror Lake, just outside the Dells, and Devils Lake, about 10 miles away, offer excellent cross-country ski trails.

We like Mirror Lake because it's such an unexpected jewel. Located just south of the Dells (the Interstate even crosses over part of the lake), Mirror Lake feels a world away. There are pines clinging to rocky walls and a surprising sense of silence.

Mirror Lake is a good choice for cross-country skiing with children, because it offers trails that are short and not too difficult. The east loop, a mile-long trail that starts near the park office, will take you through the woods and along the shore of Mirror Lake. Another short and easy loop, the beaver pond, at about .07 of a mile, will take children along a swamp where they may peek at winter animal activity—or at least some cool animal tracks.

The Dells is an easy drive from the downhill ski hills at Devil's Head and Cascade Mountain. Which one you pick depends on your family. Devil's Head, near Merrimac, features longer runs and a fast-moving quad chair lift, as well as what one 12-year-old daredevil describes as "lots of cool jumps." The lodge at Devil's Head offers some pretty reasonable deals, including an indoor pool, but the building we stayed in seemed to have seen a few too many winters of teenage ski clubs clomping through in boots.

Of course, snowboarding is the hot thing to do, and the AirPark at Devil's Head offers various attractions that sound like they'll get you to the orthopedist's office in a hurry: half-pipes, table-tops, spines, and gap jumps. For what it's worth, Devil's Head boasts 28 runs, 10 chair lifts, and a vertical drop of 500 feet.

At Cascade, boarders will find two half-pipes, two terrain parks, another speedy quad lift, a vertical drop of 460 feet, and 27 runs. Cascade also features a tubing hill for kids who would rather slide down the slopes than ski. The hill also offers a "Cascade Kids" program, that provides day care and entertainment for the little ones while Mom and Dad ski.

Which hill is cheaper? It's hard to say, because both hills offer a number of special ticket prices, so call ahead for the day you want to ski and compare.

Other Great Stuff to Do

Children who don't ski might like the Serpent Safari, one of the few Dells attractions open year round. The miniature reptile zoo is located in a shopping center in Lake Delton and features white alligators and huge snakes. See if you can get the guides to talk about the snake that nearly squeezed the owner to death. The huge skin hangs in the back, but it's not a story for children who are already afraid of snakes.

Another year-round attraction is Tommy Bartlett's Robot World. Kids can tour a replica of the Mir Space Station and play interactive science games. Unfortunately, a number of the games seemed in disrepair during a recent visit.

Don't forget Baraboo, a cute little town just 6 miles away. We like shopping around the historic Courthouse Square. Mom will like the variety of furniture stores, some featuring locally made Amish furniture, and the Shoe Box outlet store, where you can pick up some good deals on name-brand shoes, especially if you have very small or very large feet.

Kids will be attracted to Just Imagine, a very cool toy store on the north side of the square. Just Imagine features unusual toys from small manufacturers, craft and science projects, and a whole wall of Beanie Babies and their paraphernalia. There are many toys for $5 or less, making it a good spot for allowance-blowing and gift buying. We found a fun game called Frogger that kept the kids busy in the car all the way home.

Finally, you might check to see if the Mid-Continent Railway is running winter trains during your visit. The depot is in North Freedom, a few miles south of the Dells, and the historic steam locomotive rides go through the scenic Devils Lake gorge, which is just as beautiful in winter as it is in the summer.

THINGS TO SEE AND DO

Cascade Mountain Ski Area, W10441 Cascade Mountain Rd., Portage,
(608) 742-5588.

Devil's Head Ski Area, S6330 Bluff Rd., Merrimac, (800) 472-6670.

Devils Lake State Park, S5975 Park Rd., Baraboo, 53913. (608) 356-8301.

Just Imagine, 120 Fourth Ave., Baraboo, (608) 356-5507.

Mid-Continent Railway, Walnut St., North Freedom, (608) 522-4261.

Mirror Lake State Park, E10320 Fern Dell Rd., Baraboo, 53913,
(608) 254-2333.

Serpent Safari, 1425 Wisconsin Dells Parkway, Wisconsin Dells,
(608) 253-3200, www.serpentsafari.com.

Tommy Bartlett's Robot World, 560 Wisconsin Dells Parkway,
Wisconsin Dells, (608) 254-2525, www.tommybartlett.com.

PLACES TO STAY

Antigua Bay Resort and Water Park, 655 Frontage Rd., Wisconsin Dells,
(800) 54-DELLS, www.antiguabay.com.

Atlantis Hotel, 1570 Wisconsin Dells Parkway, Wisconsin Dells, (800) 800-
6179, www.dellsfun.com.

Carousel Inn, 1031 Wisconsin Dells Parkway, Wisconsin Dells,
(800) 648-4765, www.wintergreen-resort.com/carousel.

Chula Vista, 4031 N. River Rd., Wisconsin Dells, (800) 388-4782,
www.wisdells.com/chulavista.

Copacabana, 611 Wisconsin Dells Parkway, Wisconsin Dells
(800) 364-2672, www.copacabanaresort.com.

Grand Marquis Resort, 840 Wisconsin Dells Parkway, Wisconsin Dells,
(800) 447-2636, www.grandmarquis-dells.com.

Great Wolf Lodge, 1400 Black Wolf Dr., Wisconsin Dells, (800) 559-9653,
www.blackwolflodge.com.

Kalahari, 1305 Kalahari Dr., Wisconsin Dells, (877) 254-LION,
www.kalahariresort.com.

New Concord Inn, 411 Wisconsin Dells Parkway, Wisconsin Dells,
(608) 254-4338, www.dellsnewconcord.com.

Polynesian Resort, 857 N. Frontage Rd., Wisconsin Dells, (800) 272-5642,
www.dellspolynesian.com.

Raintree Resort, 1435 Wisconsin Dells Parkway, Wisconsin Dells,
(888) 253-4386, www.dellsraintree.com.

Treasure Island, 1701 Wisconsin Dells Parkway, Wisconsin Dells,
(800) 800-4997,www.wisdellstreasureisland.com.

Wilderness Resort, 511 E. Adams St., Wisconsin Dells, (800) 867-WILD,
www.wildernessresort.com.

Wintergreen Resort, 60 Gasser Rd., Wisconsin Dells, (800) 648-4765,
www.wintergreen-resort.com.

Elroy-Sparta Bike Trail

Wisconsin's oldest bike trail is also one of the best for vacationing with children. The Elroy-Sparta bike trail winds for 32 miles in west-central Wisconsin. You'll love the picturesque valleys and views of rural Wisconsin's hilly Coulee Country east of La Crosse.

Your kids will like the tunnels. Deep, dark, cool, and more than a little scary, there are three of them along the trail, marking where the railroad engineers of yore decided it was easier to burrow through the hills than go over them or around them. Thanks to the tunnels and the grade of the road, the Elroy-Sparta trail lets you explore hilly western Wisconsin without going too far afield.

Begin at Elroy

There are things to see along all 32 miles, but children tend to get restless with mere scenery to entertain them. So here are some things to talk about along the trail. Elroy, at the eastern end, is home to Tommy Thompson, Wisconsin's longest serving governor. If you ask, people will point out the modest home on the hill above Main Street where the Thompsons lived before moving to the governor's mansion. Elroy is also where you can catch the "400 Trail," which stretches south to Reedsburg, or the Omaha Trail north to Camp Douglas through the interestingly named crossroads of Hustler.

The 6 miles between Elroy and Kendall are low, marshy, and a good place to look for birds. As you get into Kendall, tell the kids to look for a red building, the old Kendall train depot that now serves as trail headquarters. It's a good spot to take a break. There are often Amish buggies with their horses tied to the hitching post across the street while the Amish shop and do their business in town. What would life be like if you were part of an Amish family?

As you leave Kendall, just where the trail crosses Highway 71, you'll see the tan brick Kendall Elementary School. This is where First Lady Sue Ann Thompson taught school for many years, even after her husband was governor. Wonder if those kids had some special field trips to Madison?

tunnel no.2 6mi
tunnel no.3 13mi
Kendall 4.5mi →
Wilton 4mi
Norwalk 9.5mi
ke flashlight

Don't forget your flashlight; you'll need it in the three old railroad tunnels along the Elroy-Sparta bike trail.

A few miles out of Kendall, you'll hit the first of three tunnels. They provide cool respite after sweaty hours on the trail. But while it might seem fun to plunge right into the darkness, it's also dangerous. Inside the tunnels, the trail has a steep drop-off, and a bike tire that goes over the edge could fling the rider into the wall. So tell kids to walk their bikes and bring flashlights, so riders coming the other way can see you.

The Tunnel Trail Campground, strategically located between tunnels one and two near Wilton, makes a good base camp. It also has those amenities that children love—a heated swimming pool and game room. Non-campers with children might like Justin Trails, a resort located about 5 miles off the trail, south of Sparta on Highway J. Accommodations include an old farmhouse for rent for large groups, a Paul Bunyan cabin, and a converted granary.

Off on the north side of the trail, you'll see a farm with large blue silos. This marks the Trailside Bed and Breakfast and the Dorset Valley School, a converted one-room school that now houses a shop offering fresh Amish bakery and crafts.

🌲 State of Confusion

If you spend time looking at the map of Wisconsin, you have to wonder if the people who named things were crazy.

Pretend you're a poor tourist looking for one of our most popular state parks, Governor Dodge State Park near Dodgeville, in Dodge County. Ha, ha. It's really in Iowa County, which is actually in Wisconsin. Got it?

If you detoured all the way east to Dodge County, you'd find that Juneau was the county seat. But you wouldn't be anywhere near the boating hotspots of Juneau County, which is in central Wisconsin along the Wisconsin River.

Juneau County is just south of Jackson County, but that's nowhere near Jackson, which is in Washington County in eastern Wisconsin. But don't look for the always popular Washington Island here. The island is off the tip of Door County in Lake Michigan, even though it's part of Wisconsin.

Confused? Washburn is the county seat of Bayfield County and a long way from Washburn County, home of the St. Croix Chippewa reservation and casino, even though it's hours north of St. Croix County. You'll also find Saukville in Ozaukee County, instead of Sauk County, where it belongs. And did you say you wanted to go to Menomonie or Menomonee Falls? Each one is several hours away from Menominee County—in opposite directions.

Don't look for Grantsburg, home of the snowmobiling-on-water championships, in Grant County or you'll be almost 300 miles too far south.

Of course, you could travel back through scenic Monroe County, where you won't find Monroe. That's the county seat of Green County, which is nowhere near Green Lake, which, unbelievably, is right where it belongs in the center of Green Lake County.

Welcome to Wilton

Your next community is the farm town of Wilton. The trail comes close to the village park, where the Kickapoo River has cut lovely rock walls. The park offers camping and a public swimming pool for cooling off after your ride. Next to the park, you'll see the Wilton Elementary School. Ask kids if they remember how far it is to Elroy. (Fifteen miles isn't that far—unless you're a little kid who has just biked it.) Then tell the kids that for many years, children in Wilton went to middle and high school in Elroy. How would they like to ride a bus that far from home everyday? In 1999, voters here decided to leave the Elroy-Kendall district and join the neighboring Norwalk-Ontario district. Villages in this part of the state are so small they join together in unified school districts.

Another favorite Wilton destination is Gina's Pies Are Square in the village of Wilton. Besides being a great pun on the mathematical formula for determining the diameter of a circle, Gina's pies really are baked in square pans and they are really good. (Try the cherry-peach, when available.) The restaurant, located in an old country store, also has a neat selection of antique knick-knacks. Children who could never be lured into antique shopping seemed unaccountably fascinated by Gina's selection of goofy salt and pepper sets, funeral home fans, and old magazines.

Norwalk

Before you get to the next town, Norwalk, the kids might notice a bad smell. It's coming from the Valley Pride meat packing plant, where cows are butchered to make hamburger meat. Kids might complain about the odor, but remind them that it's a job somebody must do. Because there weren't enough local people who wanted to work there, the plant began bringing in workers from Mexico (which is why you'll hear Spanish spoken on the streets of Norwalk). What seems like a bad job to us is a good enough job that these

The tunnels on the Elroy Sparta Trail are cool and dark, even on the hottest of summer days.

workers are willing to work far from home, sending money to support their families in Mexico.

Norwalk offers a number of good spots for treats, including Judy's Trail Cafe, where you can ride right up to the window for an ice cream cone.

The 8 miles from tunnel three to Sparta can seem like the longest part of the trip. Tell the children to watch for the beautiful Clydesdale horses at the Brookside Farms. If you look closely, you'll see that the tops of the hills have rock outcroppings that look like castles. On the steep sides of some hills, it looks like the grass is growing over a series of steps. This is where the layers of rock underneath are eroding at different rates because of the different types of rock. The rocks in this part of the state weren't plowed down by the glaciers, but are instead being worn down by water, gravity, and time.

Sparta—The End of the Trail

You'll know you've reached the trail's end when you spot Ben Biken, the 30-foot statue of a biker. Across the street is a small town treasures—an A&W restaurant that still has drive up service.

For bikers ready to cool off, follow Highway 21 east and you'll run into Memorial Park, where there's a public pool.

The Deke Slayton Memorial Bike and Space Museum is a very kid-friendly place, where admission is free, and there's a little gift shop where kids can buy a treasure for a dollar or two. It's located upstairs in the old Masonic Temple, across the street from the Monroe County Courthouse.

The museum spotlights two of Sparta's claims to fame. You can see all sorts of memorabilia from the life of the Apollo and Space Shuttle astronaut, Deke Slayton, ranging from his birth certificate (he was born in the hospital across the street) to his World War II bomber jacket. NASA lent the museum materials for a new display on the Apollo-Soyeuz joint mission of 1975.

The museum also showcases the history of the bicycle, ranging from old pushbikes to the Schwinn Black Phantom, the favorite transportation of mid-twentieth-century paperboys, to recumbent racing bikes. There's an interesting display on biker Olga McAnulty, who won the 1994 Iditasport race in Alaska, braving 200 miles of wilderness and temperatures of −25° F. Children who are very interested can actually meet McAnulty, because she runs the Out-Spokin' Adventures bike shop located just up Court Street from the Museum.

Besides guided tours and rentals, Out-Spokin' Adventures also offers shuttles to the trail. (So does the trail headquarters in Kendall.) Depending on the age of the children, one-way trips to destinations along the trail can work better than round trips. If you don't want to pay for shuttle service, kids and parents head to a destination—the public pool in Sparta or Wilton, for example. Then one parent hangs out with the kids while the other gets in the daily dose of exercise by bicycling back to get the car and pick up the kids and their bikes.

Get into Your Inner-Tube!

(Solution on page 142)

Another attraction nearby is the M&M Ranch. Its llamas, miniature horses, and wallabies are often visible from Interstate 90, and there are plenty of other things to see, including a butterfly house, parrot show, and guided farm tour. From Sparta, take Highway 16 west 5 miles to Highway J, then J south (left) through Rockland. Take the first left after the Interstate. The ranch will be on your left.

F.A.S.T. Company

A free and goofy place to visit that the kids will love is F.A.S.T, a company that churns out many of the more notable fiberglass sculptures dotting the Midwestern landscape. It's located near the Sparta end of the trail, about 2 miles northeast of town on Highway 21. (Once you pass the area's other favorite kid's attraction, the giant helicopter and tank outside the VFW Club, you're getting close.) The company's huge fiberglass sculptures, slides, and other roadside attractions include the 30-foot-tall Ben Biken, as well as the

145-foot-statue of a giant muskie in Hayward, the 55-foot-tall Jolly Green Giant in Blue Earth Minnesota, those Big Boy statues, and more. In the front, there's usually a few finished pieces awaiting shipment to parks and pools all over the world.

Out back, you can tour what seems like a fiberglass graveyard. (It's actually where they store the molds.) It's fun to see King Kong's head lying next to a giant pumpkin and an Old-Lady-in-the-Shoe from the nursery rhyme. F.A.S.T. (the name stands for fiberglass animals, signs, and trademarks) welcomes families to poke around at their own risk—but signs warn of bee and wasp nests lurking inside the molds.

A few miles beyond F.A.S.T on Highway 21, you'll enter the Fort McCoy army base. If you turn left into the main gate, then take the first right, you'll see a large brick building. This is McCoy's, a giant sports bar, restaurant, and bowling alley. Locals know it's open to the public, offering video games, virtual reality golf, and other kid-friendly attractions, perfect for a rainy day on a biking holiday.

Take in Some Bombing Practice

Central Wisconsin's other military tourist attraction is a little more unusual. About an hour northeast of Elroy is the Hardwood Gunnery Range. (From Elroy, take Highway 80 north through New Lisbon and Necedah to Finley. Turn east on Highway F, continue about 3 miles, then turn north on 11th Avenue at the Hardwood Range sign. It's about a mile to the tower and visitor viewing area.)

Strange, yes, but you can't deny the appeal of the Hardwood Gunnery Range to a certain kind of kid. (And certain grown-ups who haven't quite grown up.) After all, where else can you watch F-16s strafe the ground and B-52s drop 500-pound smoke bombs? Just . . . BLAM! BLAM! BLAM! . . . don't forget the earplugs.

The Air National Guard has been operating a bombing range here in the swampy land south of Wisconsin Rapids since 1955, the height of the Cold War. One story says the land was purchased for practice because of its resemblance to central Europe. Hardwood is one of 15 Air Guard bombing ranges in the country and one of only 4 open to the public. The planes drop dummy bombs that contain marker smoke and up to 2,000 pounds of concrete, but shoot real bullets.

Those in the know call a recording each day to find out which kind of planes are scheduled to train. On a given day, the range might host F-16s from Madison and Sioux City, B-52 bombers from Barksdale, Louisiana, or Minot, North Dakota, and C-130s from all over. Last summer, B-2 Stealth bombers trained at the range.

Visitors to Hardwood are confined to a fenced area with about seven picnic tables, a pop machine, and porta-potties. There are lots of mosquitoes and not much shade. Fancy, it is not. But that's not why people show up each day, binoculars in hand and plugs wedged into their ears. They come because they like to watch things appear to blow up.

The high-flying F-16s—barely visible specks flying at 3,000 feet—drop a line of bombs that send white smoke balls up from the range. Targets include silos, old boats, planes, buses and bulls-eyes. Up in the tower, the staff rates the pilots on accuracy.

The range operates Monday through Saturday year round, but closes for maintenance days, deer-hunting season, and during the Experimental Aircraft Association convention in Oshkosh, when there are too many planes in the air space.

It's not your normal tourist destination, but it does make for some interesting "What I did on my summer vacation" reports.

FOR MORE INFORMATION

Sparta Tourism Bureau, (608) 269-4123, www.spartawisconsin.org.

THINGS TO SEE AND DO

Deke Slayton Memorial Bike and Space Museum, 200 W. Main St., Sparta, (608) 269-0033.
Elroy-Sparta State Trail Headquarters (information and shuttle), 113 White St., Kendall, (608) 463-7109.
F.A.S.T., 14177 Highway Q (at Highway 21 East), Sparta, (608) 269-7110.
Hardwood Gunnery Range, Finley. Call (608) 427-1509 for a recorded message listing the day's scheduled training activities.
Out-Spokin' Adventures (bike rentals and shuttle), 409 Court St., Sparta, (800) 4WE-BIKE.

PLACES TO STAY

Justin Trails, 7452 Kathryn Ave., Sparta, (608) 269-4522.
Trailside Bed and Breakfast, 26147 Highway 71, (608) 435-6525.
Tunnel Trail Campground, 26983 Highway 71, Wilton, (608) 435-6829.
Wilton Village Park, Wilton, (608) 435-6132.

PLACES FOR FOOD

A&W, 100 W. Wisconsin St., Sparta, (608) 269-4844.
Gina's Pies Are Square, 400 Main St., Wilton, (608) 435-6541.
Judy's Trail Cafe, 104 Railroad St., Norwalk, (608) 823-7551.
McCoy's, 1571 S. 9th Ave., Fort McCoy, (608) 388-2065.

The Driftless Region

The southwestern part of Wisconsin, known as the Driftless Region, has so many inexpensive and convenient places to visit that it would take the family a couple of weekends to hit them all. So, we'll concentrate on a few great sites in the southern portion of the area, which is noted for its steep rocky ridges and deep ferny valleys. Thousands of years ago, glaciers that lumbered over Wisconsin spared this region, leaving its topography different from that of the rest of the state. Remember all this, in case your kids ask questions.

Governor Dodge State Park

Just looking at its the location on a map, one is initially hard pressed to see why Governor Dodge State Park is Wisconsin's third most popular state park. After all, it's far from the Great Lakes of the most popular park, Peninsula State Park, or the natural lakes of the second most popular park, Devils Lake. But what's great about it—especially for kids—is the sheer variety offered by this huge park in southwestern Wisconsin.

Spend a week at the park and you can experience the thrills of mountain biking, the clip-clop pace of trail riding on a horse, the beauty of exploring a waterfall, the mystery of an abandoned farm, and the fun of swimming in an old swimming hole. Even on a single weekend, you can accomplish many of these activities.

On a busy summer weekend, the 1,000 campers give the park the population of a small city. The 5,000-acre park easily swallows that many campers, giving the more adventurous miles of solitude even on days when the campgrounds are officially full. If the Cox Hollow Beach parking is packed when you arrive, take out the bikes and bike first, only to return to cool off later. Within five minutes, you can be all alone on the Mill Creek Mountain Bike trail.

This 3.3-mile trail makes for good skiing in the winter and fun biking for the summer. You begin by whizzing down a steep grade and across the dam that created Cox Hollow Lake. The trail is a good length for biking kids, but the little ones who lack gears on their bikes may wind up pushing up the first steep hills. If it's the right time of summer, though, the slower pace will give you a chance to pick and eat the ripe blackcap berries along the trail.

For the adventurous, this trail hooks up with the Military Ridge Trail, which can take bikers all the way to Madison, about 40 miles to the east. But the best way to tour the area is to start on the Military Ridge, because it's downhill and paved all the way from the trail into the park.

Although the Mill Creek trail starts uphill, the last part, from a spectacular view of the park's other lake, Twin Valley Lake, is downhill the entire way. Prepare to hoot and holler.

Cox Hollow is a great place to cool down after biking. It offers several kid pleasers, including a concession stand that sells everything from worms to ice cream cones. There's a shady lawn, a sand beach, and boats to rent. And older kids love to swim across the lake to several of the rock outcroppings that have rope swings. Insist that kids wear life jackets or bring floatation devices, because it is farther away from shore than it looks.

The lake also has a huge quantity of voracious blue gills and bass, and kids can even make their own poles from sticks and fishing line. A great fish story from Governor Dodge to tell kids—especially when they're swimming mid-lake—is about the unfortunate fellow who was dangling his foot in the water and was mistaken for bait by a huge muskie. More than 60 stitches were needed to repair the damage. That will make the kids swim faster!

Speaking of large animals, Governor Dodge is one of the few state parks where you can camp with your horses. The park has more than 20 miles of riding trails. If your children don't own a horse but nag for one all the time, they can still have the dude ranch experience. Doby Stables, across Highway 23 from the park, has one- and

One of the secret spots at the huge Governor Dodge State Park is Stephens Falls, a fun place to frolic in the shallow water.

105

two-hour rides. You saddle up at the stables, then ride through a tunnel under the road, and soon you're clip-clopping through the prairie grasses and cone flowers along the ridge-top trails.

For a totally different experience, you can make the short hike to Stephen's Falls, where you'll swear you've entered a tropical landscape. The half-mile trail is paved, making it accessible for wheelchairs and strollers. You'll plunge down through a ferny glade and feel the air growing cooler and moister as you near the falls. No matter how many times they visit, the kids find that the falls has a magical appeal, especially because they can clamber behind the veil of running water. For another cool spot, stop at the nearby spring house on the Meadow Valley Trail to show the kids how settlers of the dairy state kept their milk cold before refrigeration was common.

Speaking of education, Governor Dodge offers several daily ranger trips. Kids enjoy the hike to the ancient rock shelter, where they learn what life was like for people who lived in this area 1,000 years ago. Getting to handle arrowheads and other ancient artifacts is also a plus. Other programs take kids exploring caves and local wildlife. Check with the office for the daily schedule of programs. At night, there is often a talk on stars or other nature topics at the park's amphitheater.

If campfire food isn't your specialty, know that there's a whole selection of fast food restaurants on the north edge of Dodgeville, including an A&W with old-fashioned car-hop service. The Dodge Theater in downtown Dodgeville specializes in first-run family movies and, on rainy weekend nights, is often packed with campers.

Another State Park and a Cave

If the next day is a hot one, you might want to explore one of the neighboring parks, Blue Mound State Park, which is about 15 miles east on Highway 18/151. Located high atop southern Wisconsin's tallest "mountain," the 1,700-feet-tall West Blue Mound, the park is the only state park without a natural swimming lake, pond, or river. But don't despair, as it has something even better—a large, L-shaped swimming pool. If you've already purchased a yearly state park admission sticker, the pool is just 50 cents for children and $1 for adults. You can bring in lawn chairs in case all the pool's deck chairs are taken, and there is a shade arbor for those avoiding the sun. The zero-depth wading pool is a good splash area for babies and toddlers.

Nearby, on the other side of the village of Blue Mounds, the Cave of the Mounds offers respite from the heat and a tour that thousands of school children enjoy every year on their annual field trips. The cave was discovered in 1939 by local landowners blasting the limestone for a quarry. There's a quick video on how the cave was formed and an hour-long tour through the 56° F coolness. Interesting spots include the path that seems to go across deep, spike-filled water (actually a reflection of the ceiling stalactites) and the

The stalagmites and cool crystals (not to mention the cool temperature) makes the Cave of the Mounds a great stop on a summer day.

"wishing stone," the only rock in the cave that children are allowed to touch, which has stopped growing and turned white with the salt of many little hands.

On the way back to the park, stop at Betsy's Kitchen in Barneveld for malts and pie. Betsy's has an interesting history: it started as a soup kitchen to feed survivors of the 1984 Barneveld tornado.

Spring Green—
A Cultural Potpourri

If you have more of an educational or cultural bent, you might want to visit the Spring Green area, which makes for a great day trip. To start, head north on Highway 23 into the Wisconsin River Valley, past the House on the Rock. Okay, okay, we're just kidding. Stop at House on the Rock if your kids like to ogle the oddities of the world. Although not all kids will like the "don't touch" aspects of this huge collection of antiques, gimcracks, and artwork, there are things that children will like. The "giant sea creature" longer than the Statue of Liberty, the world's biggest carousel, and the "infinity room," a giant glass needle of a room that juts 218 feet over the scenic Wyoming Valley, all appeal to children's delight in "the meanest," "the biggest," and "the longest." There is, of course, one heck of a gift shop.

Let's get back to education. Just before you cross the river, you'll see the Frank Lloyd Wright Visitor Center, located in the former Spring Green restaurant, at the corner of Highways 23 and C. You can watch video tapes of the master architect's life and browse for just the Wright gift. Tours of Taliesin and the school where Wright's architects worked are available.

Across the Highway 23 bridge, you'll see the tempting sand bar of Peck's Landing. Lots of people swim and wade into the Wisconsin River here, but it's really only safe for adults or strong swimmers who are aware of the currents. One second, kids can be wading in knee deep water, while the next, they might step off the sandbar into the deep and swift current.

A better bet on the north side of the river is a stop at the Spring Green General Store, located in a brightly painted old building on Albany Street, a block off Highway 23. The store has a nifty small restaurant that features daily specials such as Indian curries and fabulous salads. Don't worry, though, there are plenty of kid's offerings, such as peanut butter and jelly and cheese quesadillas. The kid in everyone will like the cinnamon toast. A thick slice of toasted cinnamon toast comes with a side of cream cheese frosting, for a make-your-own cinnamon roll.

The General Store lives up to its name by offering an interesting selection of jewelry, house wares, and clothes. Little girls will like the inexpensive beads, hair clips, and kits for making henna designs on skin. It's tough to walk out of the General Store without eating a few goodies and carting away a few more. And, the two porches—one screened, the other open—are great spots on a rainy summer afternoon.

For high brow education, you could consider taking your children to see Shakespeare and other classic works of drama at the American Players Theater near Spring Green. The acting is so excellent, you might be surprised at your children's attention span; on the other hand, shows that run three hours can be taxing even for adults. American Players is located on the south side of the river; turn east at the Frank Lloyd Wright Visitor's Center and go about a mile to the next right and follow the signs.

Recapture Wisconsin's Lead-Mining Past

If Wisconsin history is your thing, the Driftless Region has some excellent attractions that reveal the state's proud heritage as a lead-mining center.

About 10 miles south of Governor Dodge State Park, you'll find the village of Mineral Point, and Pendarvis State Historical Site, where tour guides will explain life in the wild and woolly lead-mining days of the early 1800s. Parents will like browsing the historic shops of High Street. Children will like the Red Rooster, a small-town cafe where you can order such historic Cornish miner fare as pasties, and for dessert, figgy hobbin with caramel sauce. Another highly recommended restaurant is the Brewery Creek Inn, which offers spoofs on Wisconsin tavern food—pickled eggs and such—as well as excellent burgers, salads, and soups. The Cheese Country bike trail, connecting Mineral Point to Monroe, begins right behind the Brewery Creek.

If you are really interested in the lead-mining era, by all means head another 30 miles south to Shullsburg, another gem of a mining town. There kids can climb down into the Badger Mine, an 1827 lead mine which gave Wisconsin its nickname as the Badger State. You can take a 45-minute tour of the old mine, view a museum of mining displays and climb as far down into the 0.5-mile, hand-dug mine as your phobias will allow. The mine is part of 5 miles of tunnels that still snake beneath Shullsburg. Upstairs, you can pump the mine guide for local lore. It seems that some people in Shullsburg will still disappear down long forgotten mine shafts that reopen in their yards.

If it is Truth you want, you'll find it a few blocks away, near other streets named for the virtues of Friendship, Justice, Charity, and Hope. There are two funeral homes on Judgement Street and a church near the intersection of Truth and Judgement. The streets were named by Rev. Samuel Mazzuchelli, a Catholic missionary to lead miners and Indians and a candidate for sainthood.

Save room for lunch at the Brewster Cafe, in a cheese factory downtown. The cafe serves the traditional miner's meal of pasties—and great pies.

Old mine tailing piles from before Wisconsin was even a state are visible along roadsides around here. A rustic drive south on Highway U, then west on Highway W to New Diggings will take you past a number of old mines and tailing piles.

Of course, the strangest highway attraction in these parts is Gravity Hill. The locals say it's rediscovered by every generation of Shullsburg teenagers. Legend has it that a romantic couple who started necking in a car parked near the bottom of Gravity Hill looked up and found they had rolled back uphill into Shullsburg.

A mile or two out of town, Highway U plunges down a good-sized hill, across a low area, and curves back up a steeper hill. If you stop your car about three-quarters of the way down the first hill, just short of a 25 mph sign, Highway U appears to drop considerably to the valley floor before rising again.

But if you put the car in neutral, it will begin to roll, not into the valley in front of you but backward, so that it seems you're rolling up hill! It may not be the Big Kahuna at Noah's Ark, but natural thrills are somehow more authentic.

FOR MORE INFORMATION

General state park information: www.dnr.state.wi.us/org/land/parks.
www.springgreen.com.
www.mineralpoint.com.

THINGS TO SEE AND DO

American Players Theater, Spring Green, (608) 588-2361,
   www.americanplayers.org
Cave of the Mounds, Cave of the Mounds Rd., Blue Mounds,
   (608) 437-3038, www.caveofthemounds.com
The House on the Rock, 5754 Highway 23, Spring Green, (608) 935-3639.
   Adults (13 and over) $19.50; children 7 to 12, $11.50; 4 to 6, $5.50;
   under 3, free. www.thehouseontherock.com
Taliesin, 5607 Highway C, Spring Green, (608) 588-7900.
   www.taliesinpreservation.org.

PLACES TO CAMP

Blue Mound State Park, 4350 Mounds Park Rd., Blue Mounds,
   (608) 437-5711.
Governor Dodge State Park, 4175 Highway 23 North, Dodgeville,
   (608) 935-2315.
Tower Hill State Park, 5808 Highway C, Spring Green, (608) 588-2116.

PLACES FOR FOOD

Betsy's Kitchen, 105 Commerce St., Barneveld, (608) 924-1803.
Brewery Creek Inn, 23 Commerce St., Mineral Point, (608) 987-3298.
The Brewster Cafe, 210 W. Water St., Shullsburg, (608) 965-4485.
Red Rooster Cafe, 158 High St., Mineral Point, (608) 987-9936.
Spring Green Cafe & General Store, 137 S. Albany St., (608) 588-7070.

New Glarus

At first, New Glarus doesn't seem like a family vacation spot, but its combination of European flavor and small-town Wisconsin friendliness makes it an ideal place to spend a weekend.

You can make home base at the New Glarus Woods State Park, located high on a hill south of town. It's one of Wisconsin's smallest state parks—just an oak woods with some nature trails and playgrounds—but it has two really cool features that appeal to kids. The first is a large canvas teepee, on a wooden platform with cots, which is big enough to sleep two families (or about 10 people) and is available for rent. Kids get a kick out of camping in a teepee and parents can relax around the fire while other campers struggle with their tents.

The other cool feature is the paved spur that connects the park to the Sugar River Bike Trail. And, the really cool thing is that from the park, it's downhill all the way to New Glarus. You can just lift your feet and coast. Wheeeee!

Biking into Town

As you coast into town, even the most unobservant child will notice that the area is saturated with things Swiss, from the signs reading "Grützi!" (greetings) to the Swiss Lanes bowling alley to the Swiss Aire Motel to the Swissland Mini Golf.

The mini-golf course, across Highway 69 from the bike trail spur, is a great place to spend an hour with kids. Like everything in New Glarus, Swissland Mini Golf is fantastically tidy, and its 18 holes feature little Swiss style chalets and live goats in a hill-top enclosure that the kids can feed. Where else can you golf and feel like Heidi at the same time?

As the trail comes into downtown New Glarus, you'll stop at the old Railroad Depot, which is the headquarters for the trail that stretches 23 miles through the rolling countryside to Monticello, Albany, and Brodhead. Another planned trail will head north into Madison.

Whether it's ice cream or Swiss Cheese or fondue, New Glarus is full of snacks of the dairy variety.

You can rent bikes and use the bathroom at the depot, and in summer, the adjacent ice cream stand, the Whistle Stop Ice Cream Shoppe, is always open. If you're in need of more serious cooling off, you can head to the New Glarus public swimming pool, located in Village Park a block north of the depot. There's a diving board and a little slide for entertainment.

After your kids have cooled off, it's time for a history lesson. Tell the kids that the reason for the Swiss influence in New Glarus is that the village was founded in 1845 as a Swiss colony. At that time, poverty was rampant in Switzerland, and there wasn't enough land to support all the farmers. The canton, or state, of Glarus formed an emigration society to find new lands and they wound up in southwest Wisconsin.

Food for the Whole Family

The Swiss continue to come to the area, often to work in the area's famous cheese industry, and people here maintain their ties to the old country. If you wander in to Ruef's Meat Market, "the wurst store in town," you'll probably see copies of the latest Swiss newspapers. Ruef's is a good place to stock up on landjaeger (beef jerky type sausage) for bike trips and bratwurst to cook on your campfire.

In fact, New Glarus has so many great places to eat that it hardly seems fair. Why couldn't they be spread more evenly throughout the small towns of Wisconsin? Next door to Ruef's, the New Glarus Bakery is a must. You'll like the farmer's rye and bread sticks, and your kids will like the specialty cookies (tiny sugar cookies with fruit fillings) and homemade turtle candies.

Just down the street from the bakery, you'll find one of the favorite restaurants of the locals, The Glarner Stube. The name basically means a gathering place for the people of Glarus. Kids are welcome at this friendly place, and the dining room is a warm combination of pine and white walls. Order the fondue. Kids love to stab the bread cubes with the long forks and twirl the bread in the gooey molten cheese. Whether they actually eat any fondue is debatable, but it's worth the entertainment value alone.

The Glarner Stube has a great Friday night fish fry, sandwiches, and Swiss specialties, such as Geschnetzelets. Try saying the name three times fast. They're tender veal medallions in a cream sauce, which you will like and your kids probably will not. However, they will love the Roesti potatoes (Swiss style hash browns filled with melted cheese) and Spaetzle (little egg dumplings), so order them wherever you see them. And, depending on your level of humor, send boys into the Men's Room so they can stand in awe of what's billed as "the largest urinal in the Midwest." Yes, they sell postcards of it.

Another favorite spot is the New Glarus Hotel, built in 1853 to house the early settlers. The hotel has a pizza parlor downstairs and features fondue and other Swiss specialties in its main dining room. In the summer, you can eat on the flower-bedecked balcony. It's most fun to visit the hotel on Friday and Saturday nights, when the Roger Bright polka band puts on a dance reminiscent of small town dances of yesterday. You'll see excellent polka dancers dressed in traditional Swiss costumes, but everyone seems tolerant of beginners and kids who just want to hop from foot to foot. They play the "Chicken Dance" polka every night.

Another good eatery, owned by the same people as the hotel, is the much newer Chalet Landhaus restaurant and hotel, located next to the bike trail on Highway 69. There's a nice lounge where kids can play checkers in front of the fireplace. The dining room, decorated Swiss style with pine and white-washed walls, manages to be both warm and inviting and very, very clean. On Sunday mornings, the Chalet offers a brunch buffet, where kids can help themselves to Roesti potatoes, eggs, bacon, locally made sweet rolls, and juice. It's a great place to fuel up for a ride on the trail.

Some Other Great Biking Trails

After all the eating in New Glarus, you'll be ready to exercise. But be warned—even bike trips lead to more good food. If it's September or October, you can go on the "pie ride" to the Swiss Valley Orchard. Wind out of town north on Highway O. You'll pass Flannery's, an Irish name on a Swiss Chalet, and another good place for fish fry, and you'll pass the Wilhelm Tell Shooting Park. (Kids, can you say "Schuetzenpark"?)

On the ride, you can tell kids the story of the Swiss patriot Wilhelm Tell, who was forced by the evil rulers to shoot an apple off the head of his son. Of course, there's a lot more to the story, so if you can be in New Glarus during Labor Day weekend, check out the Wilhelm Tell Festival. The community has been performing the play since 1938—little kids here grow up from being Tell's son to being Tell to being one of the bad guys. There are cows and goats

Team Pride

```
G  H  W  G  N  I  T  A  K  S  D  E  E  P  S
I  N  O  S  C  O  N  B  S  I  B  N  T  E  A
F  M  I  C  S  A  R  A  E  T  A  S  H  E  B
R  O  S  L  K  E  S  S  T  S  S  K  E  V  H
K  E  O  C  R  E  P  K  O  R  E  C  P  H  Q
O  I  C  T  I  U  Y  E  S  E  B  U  D  I  Y
A  S  T  C  B  T  C  T  K  K  A  B  L  F  L
B  A  X  I  O  A  S  B  I  C  L  O  I  W  T
X  C  L  T  E  S  L  A  I  A  L  L  O  E  B
R  O  S  E  B  O  W  L  N  P  K  B  J  A  W
S  R  E  W  E  R  B  L  G  M  R  C  D  W  E
G  N  I  L  T  S  E  R  W  E  Y  G  A  B  R
P  U  D  Z  T  Q  W  C  P  K  E  G  U  R  C
G  O  M  M  L  K  C  U  P  R  P  Q  N  G  T
F  J  S  P  P  H  S  Y  S  Y  P  K  Q  C  R
```

BADGERS	BASEBALL	BASKETBALL
BREWERS	BUCKS	CREW
CURLING	FOOTBALL	GYMNASTICS
HOCKEY	PACKERS	ROSEBOWL
SKIING	SOCCER	SPEEDSKATING
SUPERBOWL	TRACK	WRESTLING

(Solution on page 143)

in the play which takes place outdoors. The other big event on the New Glarus calendar is the Heidi Festival, held in mid-June.

At the Swiss Valley Orchard, you'll find a large building shaped like (guess what?) a Swiss chalet that features a lunch counter where you can buy warm slices of apple pie, caramel apples, and cider.

A bike ride the other direction, south along the Sugar River Trail, will take you past the Edelweiss Chalet golf course and some lovely farm country. After about 6 miles, you'll arrive in Monticello, which has nicely restored its railroad depot as a welcome center. If you pedal into town, you'll find Gempeler's Supermarket where you can grab a snack from the deli.

Shopping Back in Town

Biking back into New Glarus, you can get a full dose of Swiss immigrant culture at the Swiss Historical Village, a collection of 14 old buildings located west of downtown on Seventh Avenue. During the summer months, costumed guides lead tours and answer questions about pioneer New Glarus.

When it's time to shop, and it's neat Swiss items you're looking for, Roberts Imports next to the large brick Swiss church offers everything from fondue pots and cowbells to fancy Swiss watches. It's the kind of place where small children might make you nervous.

It's better to take them to the Schoco-Laden, a candy and cheese shop across the street from the hotel. There you'll find Swiss chocolate and other unusual imported candies. (Who knew they made cola-flavored Gummi Bears?) You can buy ice cream cones and eat them on the bench outside, listening to polka music piped out of the bushes.

But if you love a deal, check out the Bargain Nook IV, located in the Swiss Miss Center on Highway 69. The Bargain Nooks are run by the Hodan Center, which serves disabled people in southwest Wisconsin. Much of their resale clothing is donated by Lands' End. Although some of the stuff is truly wrecked, you can find incredible bargains, such as brand new kids' felt clogs for $4 or fleece pullovers for $12.

At Close of Day

The final gastronomical attraction of New Glarus is beer, brewed locally by the New Glarus Brewery. The brewery has a small gift shop, but it's preferable to enjoy the beer in a true Wisconsin setting—the local tavern. At Puempl's (pronounced like teenage acne) Olde Tavern, you can have a spot of the local Uff-Da bock beer to wash down your limburger sandwich. The walls have historical murals of obscure Swiss historical events, and there's usually a group of old men playing the regional card game of Yass at the regular's table in front.

Speaking of limburger, you can, if you want, take your kids to the last cheese plant in America that still makes the stinky stuff. Chalet Cheese

Co-op, located about 10 miles south of New Glarus on Highway N, sells limburger and the people who work there—while urging respect for their award-winning cheese—will also tell you funny stories about people who buy it to put on the engine block of newlyweds' cars. For cheese that kids will like better, stop at Prima Käse for the sweet Swiss. It is located a few miles north of Chalet, at the intersection of Highways N and C.

If a night around the campfire at the park seems too boring after all this culture, consider making the 17-mile drive south to Monroe. The Sky Vu Drive-In, located just south of Monroe on Highway 69, is one of the last of Wisconsin's drive-in movie theaters. It also features very decent movie theater food—including homemade pizzas topped with local cheese.

You can bring your sleeping bags and lounge in the grass beneath the big screen (bring a portable radio for sound), eating pizza, and waiting for darkness and the big show.

It's a good time to practice your new command of Swiss/German words. We liked the Grützi of New Glarus and its gemütlichkeit atmosphere. We're glad they didn't shoot us with arrows when we passed the Schuetzenpark. We ate Geschnetzelets and Schnitzel and Roesti and Spaetzle. We played Yass at Puempl's. And we said "danke" to Dad when he rode up to the campsite and came back with the van to pick us up so we didn't have to ride back up the hill into New Glarus Woods.

You don't need to leave Wisconsin to learn a new language. Just say "Grützi!" and you're welcoming people in the Swiss-German dialect of the settlers of New Glarus.

THINGS TO SEE AND DO

Sky Vu Drive In, Highway 69, Monroe, (608) 325-4545.
Swissland Mini Golf, 700 Highway 69, (608) 527-5605.

PLACES TO STAY

Chalet Landhaus, 801 Highway 69, (608) 527-5234.
New Glarus Woods State Park, off Highway 69 on Highway NN,
    (608) 527-2335.
Swiss-Aire Motel, Highway 69, (608) 527-2138.

PLACES FOR FOOD

Chalet Landhaus, 8601 Highway 69, (608) 527-5234.
Glarner Stube, 518 1st St., (608) 527-2216.
New Glarus Bakery, 534 1st St., (608) 527-2916.
New Glarus Hotel, 100 6th Ave., (608) 527-5244.
Ruef's Meat Market, 538 1st St., (608) 527-2554.
Swiss Valley Orchard, Highway O, (608) 527-5355.
Whistle Stop Ice Cream, 401 Railroad St., (608) 527-5322.

PLACES TO SHOP

Anderson's Kaufhaus, 523 1st Street, (608) 527-2714.
Bargain Nook IV, 1101 Highway 69, (608) 527-3805.
Chalet Cheese Co-op, N4858 Highway N, Monroe, (608) 325-4343.
Prima Käse, W6117 Highway C, Monticello, (608) 938-4227.
Roberts Imports, 102 5th Avenue, (608) 527-2517.
Schoco-Laden, 554 1st St., (608) 527-2000.

section 4
The Northwest

Bayfield and the Apostle Islands

A note on taking children to Bayfield: they really like the Madeline Island Ferry, one of the cheapest and easiest ways to get kids out on the water to experience the Apostle Islands. But kids do not like it if, while on the ferry, their parents break into a loud and off-key rendition of, "Take me to the EYE-lands, out around Apostle EYE-lands."

Sometimes, parents can't help it. If you've been to one of the shows at the Lake Superior Big Top Chautauqua the night before, Warren Nelson's songs about the area just get stuck in your head.

Chautauqua Shows

For many families, the blue-striped Chautauqua tent, located high above Lake Superior at Mount Ashwabay (between Bayfield and Washburn) is a must stop on any trip to the Bayfield Peninsula. The Chautauqua has been bringing in national acts and producing its local shows in the big tent since 1986. The local shows, about the Apostle Island lighthouses or island life, meld original songs with cool historical slides of the area. The Chautauqua also has a few shows a year geared toward children, with jugglers and story-telling.

Whether or not kids enjoy the historical musicals depends upon the kid. Some kids are transfixed (and love it when goofy Dr. Third Eye works through the crowd, hawking his miracle waters). Other children consider black-and-white photos of anything torture and will wiggle and squirm until they have to be taken out at intermission. (Known in less culturally advanced families as "half-time.")

Kids do like running around in the grass at Chautauqua and eating the excellent pre-performance meals, which have kid-approved items such as burgers and brats, as well as a great Friday night fish boil.

Adults and kids and pets descend on Bayfield to march in the Apple Festival Parade, held the first weekend in October to celebrate the area's apple harvest. More than 50,000 visitors have been known to pack the town for the annual event. (Photo courtesy of the Bayfield Chamber of Commerce.)

The Ferry and Madeline Island

Now, back to the ferry. The other reason you will want to break out into song is that Bayfield, especially as seen from the water, is one of the loveliest towns around. White Queen Anne style homes cling to the green hillsides above the bright blue water.

Children normally have little appreciation for scenery, so tell them this about the ferry: children who live on Madeline Island take the ferry to school in Bayfield once they're in sixth grade. And in the winter, they go on a wind sled, or once the ice is solid, cars or snowmobiles. Some stay in Bayfield with friends or relatives during the school week.

The ferry ride takes just 20 minutes, the perfect length for those with short attention spans. You can either go as a passenger or with your car. Once you arrive on the dock at the Madeline Island town of La Pointe, you'll see a whole little downtown of touristy things to do.

There's a little beach in town, just south of the ferry landing. The Madeline Island Historical Museum is also in walking distance of the ferry dock. It has a cool, musical slide show that tells the history of the island, from the Ojibwa to the fur trappers to the rich folks who built summer homes here to escape the heat and treat their asthma. Go figure. The same kids who

Are We Lost?

A	B	C	D	E	F	G	H	I	J	K	L	M	N	O	P	Q	R	S	T	U	V	W	X	Y	Z
18							11						17	23			2					26			

W   W   N
26 5   19 17

W   I   S   C   O   N   S   I   N
26 11 2   18 23 17 2   11 17

N   N   I   C   O
17 24 19 9   17 11 18 23 12 19 10

O   O   I   N
12 23 23 3   11 17 13

I   S   C   O
14 11 2   18 23 22 19 15 19 14

W   S   C
5   19 26 9   2   9   18 10 6   9   12 12 7

O   C   I   N
1   23 15 18 5   11 17 9

(Solution on page 143)

121

squirmed at the Chautauqua loved the museum show. There's also a little one-room schoolhouse to explore.

You can rent bikes (and mopeds) on the island at Motion to Go and check out the islands' back roads. Because the island is 14 miles long, it's probably too much to bike the whole thing. The trip down Middle Road to Big Bay State Park (and its very nice sandy beach) is about 7 miles one way.

Big Bay State Park and Big Bay Town Park share the beach and offer about 100 campsites between them. You can (and should) reserve those at the state park; the town park takes no reservations. Besides the beach, the parks have nature trails, boardwalks over back-beach lagoons, and plenty of paved roads where kids will enjoy tooling around on their bikes. Sometimes the water is even warm enough for a brief swim.

Did we mention those lagoons? They're not only scenic, but also breed some of the biggest, meanest mosquitoes we've ever encountered. And did we mention black flies? If you're camping in mid-summer, bring bug spray, screen tents, and itch lotion.

Back in civilization (or at least island civilization), Madeline Island offers a variety of places to eat. Probably, the one kids would enjoy the most is Tom's Burned Down Cafe. It's actually a bar, but is worth a stop, if only for the story about the name (it's on the site of another business that burned down) and all the artistic and strange junk in their collection.

The Rest of the Apostles

Of course, there are 21 other Apostles to explore, the rest of them in the national lakeshore. You can most easily reach the islands by taking cruises on the Apostle Islands Cruise Service, which leaves from the same City Dock in Bayfield as the ferry. The cruise service runs a Grand Tour everyday that cruises by (but does not stop) at most of the islands. There's also a daily Is- lander cruise to Stockton Island, where kids can run on the "singing sands" that are supposed to squeak beneath their feet. There are also trips to a histo- ric fish camp on Manitou Island. The service also offers sea cave, kayak, and sailboat tours.

If you want to camp on one of the islands, the Island Shuttle will take you there. (Many of the islands have established campsites, as well as lighthouses that are staffed by volunteer lighthouse keepers, who serve as island hosts.) You need to make camping arrangements with the National Park Service.

Inside Bayfield

Back in Bayfield, the Apostle Islands National Lakeshore Visitor Center makes a good first stop in town. It's located in the old brownstone court- house at the corner of Fourth Street and Washington Avenue. After you've seen the film and the lens from the lighthouse, keep walking up the hill along Fourth Street. Take a right at Rice Avenue, and you'll be on the "iron foot-

Map Game

One player holds a map of Wisconsin and asks questions about the state. You can make up any questions that you like, but here are some to get you started.

1. Name three Wisconsin cities that begin with M.
2. What Great Lakes touch Wisconsin?
3. What other states share borders with Wisconsin?
4. If you were in Green Bay (home of the Packers) and wanted to drive to Minneapolis (home of the Vikings), which direction would you drive?
5. Which is farther north, Washington Island or Wausau?
6. Name the capital of Wisconsin and the county where it is located.
7. Which city is farther south, West Bend or La Crosse?
8. The syllables "woe" and "wau" often come from Native American names. How many Wisconsin cities sound like they were named by Native Americans?
9. Which Wisconsin counties are named for presidents?
10. If you drove north from Beloit to Minocqua, you would pass Tomahawk, Wausau, Madison, Portage, Stevens Point, and Janesville. In what order would you pass them?
11. If you drove east from Hudson to Algoma, you would pass near Wausau, Menomonie, Chippewa Falls, and Green Bay. In what order would you pass them?
12. Name Wisconsin towns that begin with directions (West Bend, South Milwaukee, etc.). Name some towns that begin with the word "New."

bridge" that takes you across a steep ravine. (One of the Chautauqua musicals, "Riding the Wind," tells about the time a huge gully washer of a storm pushed so much water down these ravines that Bayfield nearly drowned.)

On the other side of the bridge, head down Second Street and you'll soon find yourself in Bayfield's commercial district, which has enough fudge and candy shops to keep tourist-inclined children happy.

One good choice for lunch is Greunke's Restaurant. It's been in Bayfield forever, and has an old-fashioned soda fountain, a neat jukebox, and lots of Coca-Cola memorabilia. The food, especially the homemade pie, is good and there are some neat bits of local history on display. Ask them if they still have the picture of the Bayfield harbor filled with icebergs in June. And, ask the waitress if she or he was working the day the late JFK Jr. stopped in for lunch. If your children tease you for swooning over his tragic, dark handsomeness, threaten to make them eat whitefish livers.

Another fun place to eat is Maggie's, which is decorated with pink flamingos and serves pizza and burgers. For breakfast, you might want to check out the Egg Toss Cafe, which has a cool name and a screened porch.

Beyond Bayfield

If you're ready to head out of town, the hills above Bayfield are home to apple orchards and berry patches, enhancing the peninsula's reputation as the "cornucopia" region. The lake waters keep the peninsula cooler in spring, delaying fruit blossoms, and warmer in the fall, delaying the frost. Thus a number of fruit crops thrive here at the far northern tip of Wisconsin. The seasons are also much later, so if you missed the June strawberry season down south, you can still pick them here in late July. Take Highway J out of town, and you'll see signs directing you to the farms and orchards.

If you're venturing north along the peninsula, stop at the Little Sand Bay Visitor Center (you'll find it north of Highway 13, via Highway K and Sand Bay Road). There the National Park Service offers tours of an old fish camp called The Hokenson Brothers Fishery. Families can learn about the hard life of a Swedish immigrant family that made its living by lumbering, farming,

The red rocks of the Wisconsin north coast are fun to skip into the waves of Lake Superior.

and fishing. The kids might not hang on every word, but they will like clambering around the old shed and boats.

Little Sand Bay also has a beautiful and often empty beach, perfect for picnic afternoons.

Farther west along Highway 13, you'll see Meyers Road off to the right. It leads to Squaw Bay, the west edge of the Apostle Islands National Lakeshore, where there's a nice beach. Kayak tours of the sea caves launch from the shore at Squaw Bay. The tours, arranged through local outfitters such as Trek and Trail in Bayfield, are a neat thing to do with older kids, but you'll want a calm day before venturing out on the big lake with children.

Cool Cornucopia

Because kids seem to like "the biggest, the tallest, and the most," tell them that you're taking them to the farthest north town in Wisconsin. That would be Cornucopia, located north and west of Bayfield along Highway 13. Smarty-pants kids with maps will point out that some of the Apostles are farther north, but at least you can assure them that Cornucopia has the farthest north post office in Wisconsin.

To find postcards to mail to friends announcing you're truly "Up North," visit Ehlers Store. This is a true general store— a place where you can get everything from picante sauce to PVC plumbing pipe to pearl pink lipstick.

Harold Ehlers, who now runs the store, is the son of H.J. Ehlers, who started the store back in 1915 and who served for decades as Cornucopia's postmaster. He has great stories to tell about his dad.

"He had the post office back in the days when they would bring the mail in a sleigh pulled by horses, all the way from Bayfield," Ehlers said. The route is a hilly 21 miles, so just seeing the mail wagon pull into town was cause for celebration.

"Sometimes the mail was late, and if he got caught out in a storm, he'd have to spend the night at a farm," Ehlers recalled.

The postman brought news of the outside world and delivered the Cornucopia schoolteacher home to Bayfield to visit her family. Back then, the post office was a counter in the corner of the general store, where it stayed until World War II.

"My dad gave it up during the war because his three sons went into service and he didn't have enough help, so he gave up the post office and kept the store," said Ehlers, who returned home to take over the store after the war. "I told him many times he made a mistake." The post office moved to a hotel down the block, and eventually, in the1950s, to the tiny building where it is today. Kids can have their pictures snapped in front of the sign that announces "Wisconsin's Northernmost Post Office." Tell them that back in the early 1940s, people thought of changing the name of Cornucopia to North Pole. The idea was to cash in on the mail business for people who wanted packages mailed from the North Pole. But, the idea didn't catch on, and Cornucopia—named for the area's rich harvest of strawberries, raspberries, blueberries, and apples—kept its name.

"Corny," as locals call it, has a nice sandy beach with a couple of old fishing boats for kids to climb on. Close to town, you can explore Siskiwit Falls. Take Highway C to Siskiwit Falls Road. The falls are located just downstream from the bridge.

Then it will be time to go home. Because once you've been to the 54827 ZIP code, it's all down south from there.

FOR MORE INFORMATION
Madeline Island Chamber of Commerce, (888) 475-3386,
    www.madelineisland.com.
Bayfield Chamber of Commerce, 42 S. Broad St., Bayfield, (800) 447-4094.

THINGS TO SEE AND DO
Big Top Chautauqua, 101 W. Bayfield St., Washburn, (888) 244-8368,
    www.bigtop.org.
Apostle Islands Cruise Service, 119 Rittenhouse St., Bayfield,
    (800) 323-7619, www.apostleisland.com.
Madeline Island Ferry, (715) 747-2051, www.madferry.com.
Motion to Go (bicycle and moped rental), Madeline Island, (715) 747-6585.
Trek and Trail (rentals), 222 Rittenhouse Ave., Bayfield, (715) 779-3595.

PLACES TO CAMP
Big Bay State Park, P.O. Box 589, Bayfield, 54814, (715) 779-4020.
Apostle Islands National Lakeshore, 415 Washington Ave., Bayfield, 54814,
    (715) 779-3397, www.nps.gov/apis.

PLACES FOR FOOD
Greunke's, 17 Rittenhouse Ave., Bayfield, (715) 779-5480.
Maggie's, 257 Mannypenny Ave., Bayfield, (715) 779-5641.
Tom's Burned Down Café, 1 Leona Plaza, Madeline Island, (715) 747-6100.

Lake Pepin Area

Lake Pepin, in western Wisconsin roughly halfway between La Crosse and Hudson, is known for its beauty, antique shops, and boating. It could also be the start of two great literary adventures for kids.

One of them involves the lake itself, which is, of course, actually a wide section of the mighty Mississippi. It's a great place for piloting a houseboat down the river a la Mark Twain's Huckleberry Finn and Tom Sawyer. Your kids don't even have to be familiar with the stories to get excited about cruising down one of the greatest rivers in the world. But first, take them on the Laura Ingalls Wilder trip.

Discovering Laura's Legacy

Lots of women have begun the ultimate mother-daughter chick trip near here. Wisconsin children who know and love the "Little House on the Prairie" also know that Laura Ingalls Wilder was born in Wisconsin and that the first book in the series, "Little House in the Big Woods," was set here. Northern Wisconsin is where Laura's grandparents introduced her to the treat of "sugar snow," warm maple syrup poured on fresh snow, and where Laura and Ma saw a bear in their yard one snowy night.

Laura's story, that of pioneers who tried their fate along the frontier, takes her family from the Big Woods of Wisconsin to the prairies of Minnesota, Iowa, Kansas, and South Dakota.

Many a mixed age group of readers have begun their Laura quest here in Pepin, which bills itself as the start of the Laura Ingalls Wilder Highway. Maps to all the Laura sites can be found at either the Pepin Historical Museum (open May to October) or at the Mabel Tainter Memorial Theater (open year round) in Menominee. If you start the trail in Menominee, you can also visit the home of another girl pioneer of literature, Caddie Woodlawn.

Laura Ingalls Wilder was born in 1867 in a small cabin about 7 miles up a steep valley near the crossroads village of Lund. A replica cabin has been built along Highway CC, where you can have picnics and peek into the windows.

Land of 15,000 Lakes

```
W  E  S  A  U  B  A  S  B  N  L  F  I  S  L
V  I  E  J  F  I  F  U  F  E  A  L  E  E  G
N  E  N  K  A  H  T  O  E  B  U  G  E  F  V
B  F  E  N  U  T  N  M  K  A  W  S  G  H  D
G  W  Y  U  E  A  F  P  I  G  E  H  T  N  S
L  E  Q  R  W  B  W  A  P  A  F  Z  I  D  E
H  R  N  A  Y  G  A  E  L  M  K  W  E  H  L
W  U  H  E  Y  F  Y  G  P  O  K  V  G  C  K
T  S  F  Z  V  A  A  M  O  N  I  H  J  Z  A
S  T  A  R  G  A  B  P  E  L  I  C  A  N  R
E  N  O  T  S  D  E  R  S  B  T  U  O  R  T
B  X  A  L  X  L  U  I  X  L  G  A  Y  D  Y
V  O  Y  E  B  D  Q  I  P  L  F  S  U  C  V
L  A  N  H  X  K  O  S  H  K  O  N  O  N  G
I  H  Z  E  P  K  N  R  D  O  K  L  W  K  Y
```

BONE	BUTTERNUT	DEVILS
ELKART	GENEVA	KOSHKONONG
NEBAGAMON	NOQUEBAY	PELICAN
PEWAUKEE	PIKE	REDSTONE
SHAWANO	SHELL	STAR
TROUT	WIND	WINNEBAGO

(Solution on page 143)

Bring along the book, and you can read about Laura, baby Carrie, and the bears and panthers of wilderness Wisconsin. You'll have to use your imagination, though, because the big woods have long since been replaced with farm fields.

Down in the Mississippi River town of Pepin, you'll find a fuller display about Laura and her life at the Pepin Historical Museum. Her books and other gift items are available in the museum.

True Laura fanatics will want to visit the third weekend in September, when Laura Ingalls Wilder Days includes a Laura-Look-Alike contest, a parade, storytelling, a theater production, and a frontier encampment with period crafts and demonstrations.

Other Pepin Area Attractions

The Lake Pepin area is home to fabulous scenery, quaint inns, fancy restaurants, and antique stores galore—none of which hold much attraction for children.

It is, however, possible to trick children into enjoying the scenery. If your children like slightly gruesome (and probably untrue) stories, take them to the lookout at Maiden Rock, about 15 miles upstream from Pepin. There, legend has it, the beautiful Indian maiden Winona threw herself off the bluff into the river when her father refused to let her marry her love. Even if it's not true, your kids will always remember how Winona, Minnesota, and Maiden Rock, Wisconsin, got their names.

At Maiden Rock bluff, you can also challenge your children to look north and west across the Mississippi to see if they can pick out the optical illusion of "Point-No-Point" on the Minnesota side. Old river boat pilot Mark Twain has written about looking for the landmark point then seeing it "mile away and fold back into the bank."

Sometimes children appreciate nature if they have to work for their view. With that in mind, try the steep climb up "Bogus Bluff" near the site of old Fort Antoine, between Pepin and Stockholm. It's a good place to have a geology lesson about how Lake Pepin was formed. The vigorous Chippewa River dumps so much rock and other debris when it flows into the slower moving Mississippi that it creates a natural dam across the larger river, creating Lake Pepin and a great place for windsurfing, sailing, and other opportunities.

Children who don't mind sitting might like the entire 70-mile "circle tour" of Lake Pepin, which includes river crossings at Red Wing and Wabasha. The village of Stockholm has an impressive number of shops and galleries, especially considering that the population is less than 100 souls. Mothers and *some* kids will love the shopping, so be prepared to take the anti-shopping contingent on a walk to Village Park.

If your children are adventurous eaters, by all means take them to the Harbor View Cafe in Pepin. You'll know you're close when you can smell the garlic. The cafe has a neat dining room lined with books, and specializes in interesting takes on local delicacies. One spring, the special was morel mushrooms and wild asparagus on toast. The cafe also has a children's menu. Another family-friendly restaurant in Pepin is the Park View Cafe.

Houseboating on the Mississippi

Of course, you can also arrive at the Harbor View and Lake Pepin by boat. The Mississippi River is home to another great literary adventure—the Huck Finn houseboat adventure. (In fact, one of the many boat rental places along the river is called Huck's Houseboats, which has a dock in La Crosse. It rents boats with amenities that old Tom and Huck never dreamed of: air conditioning, refrigerators, and waterslides for splashing down into the Mississippi.)

A family vacation aboard a Mississippi houseboat is a chance to poke along the river at your own speed. You can dock in towns like Pepin for dining and amenities, or head into the wilderness of the sloughs to check out bald eagles, pelicans and other river birds.

It's not cheap—a week on a deluxe houseboat will set you back about $1,500; a weekend trip is about $1,000. But rates (and bug populations) drop

Rent a houseboat from one of the many marinas along the Mississippi River and you'll have the freedom to wander and the comforts of home. You'll also learn to beach at hospitable-looking sandbar islands.

after Labor Day. And the rental places say that their boats are so simple, you can maneuver one even if you don't know how to steer a rowboat. Really?

Actually, it is pretty easy. The marina crew will show you how to raise and lower the motor, and to learn the lag time between turning the wheel and when the boat responds. The Mississippi's main channel is marked so clearly that staying between the buoys is practically mindless. The only time you have to study the river with the concentration of one of Mark Twain's riverboat pilots is when you venture out of the channel. But venture out you should, because docking at a sandbar (using huge anchors that look like something out of a Popeye cartoon) is when you really enjoy the river.

Although the bluffs you see from the main channel are beautiful, the real charm is in the backwaters. Anchor early so you can find a beach spot without many people, because the river is a busy place most summer weekends.

You can fish and swim right off the boat. If you're lucky enough to have a waterslide houseboat, you can climb to the upper deck, turn on the water, and let it rip. It's a good idea to explore the area first to make sure that the water is deep enough and that there are no sunken trees or other obstructions below your slide. You should probably also make kids wear lifejackets.

Before dark, gather wood for a big campfire to keep the bugs away. Although kids might nag to camp on the island, it's hard to want to sleep in a tent when comfortable, bug-free bunks await.

Many of the boats come with smaller craft (ranging from kayaks to jon boats) for exploring the backwaters, a great way to see the creatures of the Mississippi—snapping turtles, cormorants, and paddlefish. In a few minutes you can leave the "party boat" scene behind, and enjoy sunset on a calm slough with great horned owls and sandhill cranes for company.

Kids learn a lot on trips like this—including the bad words daddy says when he bashes the boat into a dock. Seriously, though, after the experience of going through the locks, kids will understand how they work to raise and lower boats, and how the Upper Mississippi is really a series of linked pools.

Barges look a lot more impressive when you're in your small boat, sharing the channel with them. A full "tow" contains 15 barges and is a quarter mile long. At night, you can see the searchlight that the pilot keeps trained on the far end of the barge.

The nice thing about a river adventure is that you can stop whenever and wherever you like. Trempealeau, Fountain City, and Pepin are fun to explore. How far you cruise depends on how much time you have. One marina estimates that you can cover 250 cruising miles in a week—roughly the distance from Lansing, Iowa to Winona, Minnesota, and back—in a week. Figure about half of that for a three-day weekend.

You might want to plan your trips around area festivals. Besides Laura Ingalls Wilder Days, river towns host Sunfish Days in Onalaska in late May,

Was it like this for Tom and Huck? You'll easily master the pace of life on the Mississippi aboard your own sailboat.

RiverFest in La Crosse, Catfish Days in Trempealeau in July, and Oktoberfest in La Crosse in late September or early October.

Besides houseboats and hotels, there is camping available at Lake Pepin Campground, Riv-Way Campground in Pepin, and the Stockholm Village Park in Stockholm.

Biking and Cave Exploring

Once your children have had enough of the river, you can head up to the bike trails that follow the Red Cedar and Chippewa Rivers. It is possible to start in Menominee and ride down the Red Cedar River, then back up the Chippewa River all the way to Cornell. But we've found that, with children, less is usually more. The 14-mile Red Cedar Trail offers a lot of scenery along a distance right for most school-aged children.

You can start in Menominee, at the parking lot in Riverside Park. Once you're out of town, look for the weeping rock wall, covered with aqua-colored ice in the cold months. It is about 6 miles to Downsville, where there are restaurants and a picnic area. Once you're past Downsville, look for the old stone quarry, a fun place to explore. And if you make it to the trail's junction with the Chippewa River State Trail, you'll be able to check out the wetland views from a 900-feet-long railroad trestle.

Another good kid pleaser in the area is the Crystal Cave in Spring Valley, the state's longest cavern, which is open for tours from April to October. The cave is located in one of Wisconsin prettiest areas, not far from Nugget Lake and Plum City. Nugget Lake is an old meteor crater and was once the site of gold and diamond mining. You may want to lure children into a hike around one of the county park trails with the bait of finding precious jewels.

Check Out the UFOs

Speaking of meteors and things from outer space, kids might like to visit Elmwood, which bills itself as The UFO Capital of Wisconsin. The local celebration is UFO Days, held the last full weekend of July, which includes a parade and other activities.

The name dates back to 1975, when a local resident and her three children noticed a particularly bright "star" while driving home. The object stayed alongside their car as they drove, and tried to land in front of her car. The kids were screaming and crying, and she was honking as she drove. The object rose in the air above the trees, but was still visible, with lights glowing an orange color, to the neighbors when they came out of the house to investigate. In another sighting, a local police officer, George Wheeler, saw a "flaming ball the size of a football field" that struck his squad car. The car needed a change of plugs and points; both had been burned out. Later Wheeler would say, "I don't know what I saw, but all I know is that I don't want that experience again."

So, this is a third kind of literary adventure near Wisconsin's west coast. Kids who aren't taken with classics, such as "Huckleberry Finn" or "Little House in the Big Woods," might like a vacation based on science fiction.

FOR MORE INFORMATION

Pepin Visitor Information Center, (715) 442–3011, Pepin Area Community
  Club, www.pepinwisconsin.com.

THINGS TO SEE AND DO

Crystal Cave, 965 Highway 29, Spring Valley, (715) 778-4414.
Laura Ingalls Wilder Information Center, Mabel Tainter Theater, 205 Main
  St., Menomonie, (715) 235-9726.
Red Cedar Bike Trail, (800) 283-1862 (Menomonie Visitors Center).

HOUSEBOAT RENTALS

Fun 'n Sun Houseboats, La Crosse, Trempealeau, and Winona, Minnesota,
  (888) 343-5670, www.funsun.com.
Great River Houseboats, 1009 E. Main St., Wabasha, Minnesota,
  (651) 565-3376, www.greatriverhouseboats.com.

Huck's Houseboats, La Crosse, (800) 359-3035, www.hucks.com.

S & S Houseboat Rentals, 990 S. Front St., Lansing, Iowa, (800) 728-0131, www.ssboatrentals.com.

PLACES TO STAY

Nugget Lake Park (about 55 campsites), N4351 County Road HH, Plum City, (715) 639-5611.

Bumble Bee Campground, 200 Washington St., Pepin, (715) 442-2592.

PLACES FOR FOOD

Harbor View Cafe, Pepin, (715) 442-3893.

Park View Cafe, 809 3rd St., Pepin, (715) 442-4202.

Trempealeau

If you ask parents who spent a weekend at Trempealeau to recall their most treasured moments, they would probably talk about sitting in the Adirondack chairs on the deck of the historic Trempealeau Hotel, enjoying their coffee while watching the mighty Mississippi flow in front of the green bluffs of the Minnesota side. And if you ask the kids? Well, they loved the snakes and cigarettes.

Trempealeau with Kids

You may wonder whether or not to take the youngsters to Trempealeau, one of our favorite child-free weekend destinations. Like neighboring towns on this stretch of the river, with their old brick buildings tucked up against the towering bluffs, Trempealeau has an end-of-the-earth feeling. At the same time, the constant barge traffic reminds you that the Mississippi is the water highway down the heart of America. It's easy to feel connected to the cities of New Orleans and Minneapolis while sipping your coffee at the end of the earth.

With its marina and Great River Bike Trail, Trempealeau is a natural base camp for recreational vacations on the Mississippi. Perrot State Park and the Trempealeau National Wildlife Refuge are just outside of town. On summer weekends, Trempealeau buzzes with bicyclists and bikers, boaters, and bird-watchers from three states.

You can take a great hiking tour in Perrot State Park, just north of town, so the kids could experience the tremendous views from the "goat prairies" on top of the bluffs. But because of the biting insects that thrive in the river backwaters, you may want to look elsewhere for sleeping accommodations when night falls.

Likewise, adults will enjoy staying at the Trempealeau Hotel, a historic treasure founded in 1871, while enjoying the outdoor music at its "Bluesfest" and "Reggae Sunsplash" weekends. But the "European style" rooms are barely big enough for a double bed; the lack of private bathrooms and cable TV will probably mean that you would be better off staying elsewhere with children.

There's the Pleasant Knoll Motel, for example, a family-run place three blocks up the hill, with large and neat rooms (children under 12 stay free).

Lots to Do in La Crosse

Keeping close to the Mississippi River, you'll want to venture 18 miles south to La Crosse, with a stop at the new Gertrude Salzer Gordon Children's Museum of La Crosse. The museum opened in March 1999 to incredible business—drawing 20,000 visitors in its first two months. It occupies three spacious floors of a former furniture store, at 207 South Fifth Avenue, in downtown La Crosse. Unlike most children's museums, which tend to appeal to the smallest of children, this one had enough attractions to enthrall our 8- and 11-year-old children.

Campers at Perrot State Park have views of Trempealeau Mountain, which the French explorers named to mean "Mountain soaking in water."

The biggest attraction is truly big—the three-story high "Mount Le Kid" climbing wall. Children are helmeted and strapped into a rope harness. Then, as museum volunteers hold them on belay, the kids can clamber up the vertical wall, finding toe and finger holds on the protruding "rocks." Kids love it, but it's only open when there are volunteers to staff it, generally on the weekends.

Another big favorite is the "Mighty Mississippi" display—two meandering water tables that recreate the Mississippi River between the Black River and Genoa, with flowing water and scale models of local landmarks such as Granddad's Bluff. In the 1890's version of the river, children can send miniature logs running—and sometimes jamming—down the natural river course of the era. The other table portrays the modern Mississippi, with its dams, levees, and locks. Children race boats down the river and can operate two sets of locks, raising and lowering their boats between levels of the managed river. They love this activity—and it helps them understand what they can later see in Trempealeau.

The museum also offers a maze, a real fire truck, a creative arts room, a farm for toddlers, and "Grandma's Attic," where dressers and wardrobes full of costumes invite children to dress up and put on a play. There's also a beat-

State Park Puzzler

```
P  K  Y  E  L  L  O  W  S  T  O  N  E  I  H
I  C  K  B  O  J  A  W  F  P  K  H  N  H  I
K  I  K  B  T  O  S  F  N  D  E  T  Q  R  G
E  R  D  M  Z  W  U  E  I  Y  E  R  U  I  H
L  R  Q  J  Z  L  W  O  O  R  X  R  O  T  C
A  E  R  P  B  P  K  I  S  R  W  V  Z  T  L
K  M  D  L  O  W  F  T  O  E  Y  Z  I  B  I
E  E  L  R  N  I  A  C  P  N  A  J  D  X  F
H  I  T  X  F  T  K  B  A  C  L  P  K  X  F
M  U  J  X  E  I  I  J  T  T  U  P  Y  J  S
A  X  A  M  S  G  B  B  T  U  S  M  D  T  D
S  F  T  L  F  V  R  K  I  D  I  C  W  E  C
Q  E  A  O  N  F  B  Y  S  N  N  W  N  S  A
Y  N  O  O  X  U  W  H  O  E  G  Q  T  W  H
D  T  Z  S  Y  G  S  W  N  Y  A  B  G  I  B
```

BIGBAY	BIGFOOT	HIGHCLIFF
INTERSTATE	MERRICK	MILLBLUFF
NEWPORT	PATTISON	PEROT
PIKELAKE	ROCKISLAND	WYALUSING
YELLOWSTONE		

(Solution on page 143)

🌲 Wisconsin Waterfalls

Take a map of Wisconsin and draw a line connecting the names of Central Wisconsin Cities that have "Falls" or "Rapids" in the name. You'll have a curving line connecting Chippewa Falls, Black River Falls, Wisconsin Rapids, Big Falls, and Oconto Falls.

Why? The line marks the places where rivers flowing south plunge off the hard rock of the "Canadian Shield" and down into the plain of central Wisconsin. The waterfall towns were good places to build lumber mills and paper mills because of the waterpower supplied by the rivers. These are not the state's biggest waterfalls, however.

You can make another line farther north that connects Wisconsin's biggest waterfalls: Big Manitou Falls in Pattison State Park, Amnicon Falls, Copper Falls, and Peterson Falls, Superior Falls, and Potato Falls in Iron County. These falls are generally more spectacular than those farther south. Big Manitou Falls near Superior, at 165 feet, is the fourth highest waterfall east of the Rockies. By way of comparison, Niagara Falls is 182 feet on the Canadian side.

The northern Wisconsin waterfalls mark where rivers flowing north plunge off the Canadian Shield and down into the Lake Superior lowland.

ing heart children can walk through, as well as a playhouse, giant building blocks, and a theater. Plan on spending several hours.

Hungry after all that play, you can head to Piggy's, 328 Front Street, a restaurant located right on the Mississippi. Ask for the window seats that provide prime viewing of all the water sports. While you enjoy the excellent smoked chicken and blackened orange roughy, children can be kept entertained by the passing show on the river. You can watch the swimmers at Pettibone Beach on the island in the middle of the channel. In the summer, jet-skiers whiz by, and the *Island Girl*, a cruise ship that sails regularly around the island, will float into view, along with an endless parade of houseboats and speedboats. If you're lucky, you'll catch sight of a barge—as wide as two football fields and as long as five—slowly passing. The Mississippi's mix of the industrial and the recreational makes it endlessly entertaining. And when the children get tired of watching boats, they'll enjoy the giant muskrats, that run in and out of the grass below the windows.

Piggy's is justly known for its smoked prime rib and barbecued ribs, but it also has a very nice children's menu, featuring barbecued chicken and fries, burgers, and grilled cheese sandwiches.

You'll be full after dinner, but should still check out The Pearl, 207 Pearl Street, a 1930s vintage ice cream parlor tucked into a restored building in downtown La Crosse. All the goodies, especially the banana splits and ice cream sodas, are great. But the children should be drawn, as ours were, to the large glass cases of novelty candies. Although the "old-fashioned" candy was familiar from our baby boom youth, our kids had never experienced the thrill of wax lips, tiny wax bottles filled with syrup, and candy buttons on rolls of white paper. They had especially never seen chocolate cigarettes—so, political correctness be damned—we let them each buy a pack. The big red lips and cigarettes kept them busy clowning all the way to Trempealeau.

On the trip back, one of the sites that should keep the youngsters occupied for a time is the observation deck of Lock and Dam Number 6, which will allow them to put their new knowledge of locks to work. They can watch the big barges get lowered from pool Number 6 above Trempealeau to the lower river.

Trempealeau Wildlife Refuge

The Trempealeau National Wildlife Refuge marks the beginning of the Great River State Trail. From here, you can ride 27 miles to the La Crosse River Trail, then the Elroy-Sparta Trail, then the 400 Trail, and ride 117 miles all the way to Reedsburg. This is way beyond the ability of most families, so you may decide to bike the paved and gravel roads of the wildlife refuge itself, where you can meet pelicans, cranes, and multiple herons. We started seeing wildlife before we even got out of the car. We slowed to examine a baby snapping turtle and a larger box turtle crossing the road, and stopped again when we saw a snapper the size of a platter in the grass. (Another option is to paddle the marked Long Lake Canoe Trail through the refuge; bike and canoe rentals are available at the Trempealeau Hotel.)

To bike through the lowlands of the refuge is to appreciate how the Upper Mississippi resembles the bayous farther down river. The woods buzz, hum, and croak with animal life, and you almost expect to see alligators slithering into the water. You can peddle to the diversion dike that leads out to the area's namesake, Trempealeau Mountain. The name is French for "mountain standing in the water;" in actuality, it's a tall bluff that got stranded out in the water by a change in the course of the Mississippi.

While we were thrilled to see so many egrets and herons—bring binoculars—the kids were fascinated by the wildlife right at their feet. The rocks on the sunny side of the dike make great nests and sun bathing spots for several varieties of snakes, including bull snakes as fat as broom handles The kids were especially thrilled to find two recently shed snake skins, their favorite souvenirs of the trip. The dike ends at Trempealeau Mountain, but trails lead into the woods for those who want to explore the effigy mounds and the mountain itself.

Sunset lights the water of the Mississippi River at Trempealeau. Can the mosquitoes be far behind?

Back in Town

Returning to home base at the Trempealeau Hotel, you can relax or, as we did, play sand volleyball in the yard while waiting for some food. The yard is also a great place to watch boat traffic and the freight trains that roar by just on the other side of the picket fence. Eating out on the screen porch gives you an opportunity to mingle with many other families. The adults in the group loved the catfish sandwich with garlic mayonnaise, while the children were happy with grilled chicken strips, tortilla strips, and 1919 Root Beer on tap. This was a peaceful ending to a great river adventure, and on the way home, we plotted our return to the river in a houseboat.

THINGS TO SEE AND DO

Custom Canoe Trips, c/o Trempealeau Hotel Trading Post, Trempealeau Hotel, 150 Main St., Trempealeau, (608) 534-6898.

Gertrude Salzer Gordon Children's Museum of La Crosse, 207 S. 5th Ave., La Crosse, (608) 784-2652.

Island Girl river cruises, 621 Park Plaza Dr., La Crosse, (608) 784-0556. www.greatriver.com/islandgirl/cruises.htm.

La Crosse Doll Museum, 1213 Caledonia St., La Crosse, (608) 785-0020.

Myrick Park, 2000 La Crosse St., La Crosse, (608) 789-7533.

Perrot State Park, P.O. Box 407, Sullivan Rd., Trempealeau, (608) 534-6409.

The Rock in the House, 440 N. Shore Dr., Fountain City, (608) 687-6106.

Trempealeau Marina, Lock and Dam Number 6, (608) 534-6033.

Trempealeau National Wildlife Refuge, W28488 Refuge Road, Trempealeau, (608) 539-2311.

PLACES TO STAY

Pleasant Knoll Motel, 11451 Main St., Trempealeau, (608) 534-6615, www.greatriver.com/pleasantknoll/welcome.

Riverview Motel, Main and First Streets, Trempealeau, (608) 534-7784. E-mail: Rivervw@win.bright.net.

Trempealeau Hotel, 150 Main St., Trempealeau, (608) 534-6898, www.greatriver.com/hotel.htm.

PLACES FOR FOOD

Ed Sullivan's, on the Mississippi at the south entrance to Perrot State Park, (608) 534-7775.

Piggy's, 328 Front St., La Crosse, (608) 784-4877.

The Pearl, 207 Pearl St., La Crosse, (608) 782-6655.

Trempealeau Hotel, 150 Main St., Trempealeau, (608) 534-6898.

Wild Wisconsin Rivers
(Puzzle from page 17)

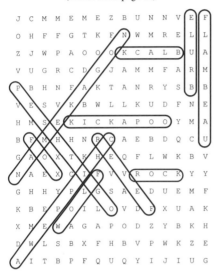

Fun Up North
(Puzzle from page 31)

In the Dells
(Puzzle from page 91)

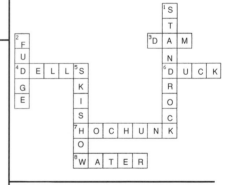

Vacation Advice
(Puzzle from page 66)

Get into Your Inner-Tube!
(Puzzle from page 101)

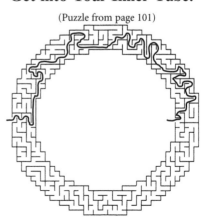

Team Pride

(Puzzle from page 114)

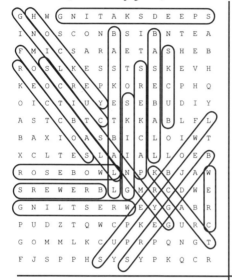

Land of 15,000 Lakes

(Puzzle from page 128)

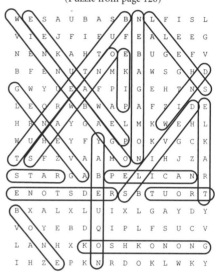

Are We Lost?

(Puzzle from page 121)

WHEN JEAN NICOLET DISCOVERED WISCONSIN HE WAS ACTUALLY LOOKING FOR CHINA

State Park Puzzler

(Puzzle from page 137)

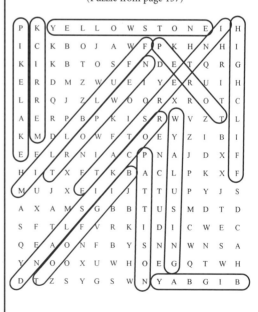

Index

More Great Titles from Trails Books

ACTIVITY GUIDES

Wisconsin Underground: A Guide to Caves, Mines, and Tunnels in and around the Badger State
Doris Green

Paddling Illinois: 64 Great Trips by Canoe and Kayak
Mike Svob

Paddling Northern Wisconsin: 82 Great Trips by Canoe and Kayak
Mike Svob

Great Minnesota Walks: 49 Strolls, Rambles, Hikes, and Treks
Wm. Chad McGrath

Great Wisconsin Walks: 45 Strolls, Rambles, Hikes, and Treks
Wm. Chad McGrath

Best Wisconsin Bike Trips
Phil Van Valkenberg

TRAVEL GUIDES

The Great Wisconsin Touring Book: 30 Spectacular Auto Tours
Gary Knowles

County Parks of Wisconsin, Revised Edition
Jeannette and Chet Bell

Up North Wisconsin: A Region for All Seasons
Sharyn Alden

The Spirit of Door County: A Photographic Essay
Darryl R. Beers

Great Wisconsin Taverns: 101 Distinctive Badger Bars
Dennis Boyer

Great Wisconsin Restaurants
Dennis Getto

Great Weekend Adventures
the Editors of Wisconsin Trails

The Wisconsin Traveler's Companion: A Guide to Country Sights
Jerry Apps and Julie Sutter-Blair

HOME AND GARDEN

Creating a Perennial Garden in the Midwest
Joan Severa

Bountiful Wisconsin: 110 Favorite Recipes
Terese Allen

Foods That Made Wisconsin Famous
Richard J. Baumann

HISTORICAL GUIDES

Walking Tours of Wisconsin's Historic Towns
Lucy Rhodes, Elizabeth McBride, and Anita Matcha

Wisconsin: The Story of the Badger State
Norman K. Risjord

Barns of Wisconsin
Jerry Apps

**Portrait of the Past: A Photographic Journey
Through Wisconsin, 1865–1920**
Howard Mead, Jill Dean, and Susan Smith

FOR YOUNG PEOPLE

Wisconsin Portraits: 55 People Who Made a Difference
Martin Hintz

ABCs of Wisconsin
Dori Hillestad Butler and Alison Relyea

W Is for Wisconsin
Dori Hillestad Butler and Eileen Dawson

OTHER TITLES OF INTEREST

The I-Files: True Reports of Unexplained Phenomena in Illinois
Jay Rath

The W-Files: True Reports of Wisconsin's Unexplained Phenomena
Jay Rath

The M-Files: True Reports of Minnesota's Unexplained Phenomena
Jay Rath

For a free catalog, phone, write, or e-mail us.

Trails Books
P.O. Box 317, Black Earth, WI 53515
(800) 236-8088 • e-mail: info@wistrails.com
www.trailsbooks.com